Oct 5, 1990

To Dirnk & Tany:

Words can't express
how much Anne & I
treasure your friendship
& loyalty!

Sincerely
Bob Woolf

FRIENDLY
PERSUASION

"In this most informative book, Bob Woolf sets forth his formula for negotiating. It is, in fact, more than a formula for negotiating, it is a formula by which everyone can live, work and succeed."

—SENATOR GEORGE MITCHELL
US Senate Majority Leader

"Mr. Woolf has negotiated all my contracts since Day 1, and I couldn't be happier."

—LARRY BIRD
Boston Celtics

"Bob Woolf is a superstar negotiator. If he were a movie, he would run away with all the Oscars—for Best Actor; Best Director; Best Supporting Actor and Best Screenplay—and of course, Best at the Box Office."

—GENE SHALIT
NBC *Today Show*

"For over twenty years Bob Woolf has negotiated for me. He knows how to get the job done in a way that is fair to everyone."

—CARL YASTRZEMSKI
Baseball Hall of Fame

"Bob Woolf is a great negotiator with strong principles, and I truly enjoy working with him on behalf of New Kids on the Block."

—DICK SCOTT
Manager
New Kids on the Block

"I've been on two championship teams—the Los Angeles Lakers and with Bob Woolf. He is the world champion of negotiators."

—BYRON SCOTT
Los Angeles Lakers

"If they gave trophies for negotiating, Bob Woolf would win the Heisman."

—VINNY TESTAVERDE
Tampa Bay Buccaneers

"Bob Woolf has negotiated my way through the difficult world of professional sports, for which I am grateful—every college athlete and student should read this book."

—DOUG FLUTIE
Heisman Trophy Winner

"This book should be required reading for every business and law school student in the world. Bob Woolf's negotiating techniques and Golden Rule approach to negotiating really work. Nice guys can finish first, if they use Woolf's technique."

—PROFESSOR ALAN DERSHOWITZ
Harvard Law School

"Reading Bob Woolf's book only confirmed why I chose him to negotiate for me."

—DON MAJKOWSKI
Green Bay Packers

"When my career was at a crossroads, Bob Woolf came forward and negotiated a contract that only he could have handled."

—BERNARD KING
Washington Bullets

"This book is totally valid today and will be just as valid 1,000 years from now."

—RICHARD BOONISAR
Chairman of the Board
(Retired)
Sheraton Corporation of America

"Bob Woolf provides invaluable insights into the art of negotiating."

—J. W. MARRIOTT, JR.,
Chairman & President,
Marriott Corporation

"Take my advice. Read this book and use Bob Woolf's hard-earned knowledge. He knows what he's talking about."

—TED TURNER
Turner Broadcasting System

"Bob Woolf is an amazing negotiator and a super human being—he is pure magic."

—SIDNEY GREEN
Orlando Magic

"Bob Woolf is a patient and caring man and has been like a father to me. I've always followed his advice—after reading this book, you'll know why."

—JIM CRAIG
Olympic Hockey Goalie

4

"On the court I listen to my coach and my instincts; off the court I listen to Bob Woolf."

—SEAN ELLIOTT
San Antonio Spurs

"The sooner you read this book, the sooner you will become a better negotiator."

—F. LEE BAILEY, ESQ.

"No one has been involved in more big deals in sports over the past twenty-five years than Bob Woolf, and in almost every instance he has come away a winner. This book should serve as a primer for anyone who considers himself a budding attorney, entrepreneur or successful businessman."

—WILL MCDONOUGH
NBC Sports commentator
Columnist, *The Boston Globe*

"If I could choose one person to run my life as well as my work, it would be Bob Woolf. That is what I concluded after reading his book *Friendly Persuasion: My Life As a Negotiator*."

—DAVID BROWN
Film producer of *Jaws*, *The Verdict*, *The Sting*, *Cocoon*, and *Driving Miss Daisy*

"When all you ever wanted wasn't enough, Bob Woolf can get it for you. He's one of the very best, and his Rolodex proves it!"

—HARVEY MACKAY
Author of the bestselling *Swim With the Sharks Without Being Eaten Alive*

FRIENDLY PERSUASION

My Life As a Negotiator

BOB WOOLF

G. P. Putnam's Sons
NEW YORK

G. P. Putnam's Sons
Publishers Since 1838
200 Madison Avenue
New York, NY 10016

Photos not otherwise credited come from Bob Woolf's personal collection.

Library of Congress Cataloging-in-Publication Data

Woolf, Bob, date.
      Friendly persuasion : my life as a negotiator / Bob Woolf.
          p.   cm.
      ISBN 0-399-13552-9
      1. Negotiation.   2. Persuasion (Psychology)   3. Woolf, Bob, date.
      I. Title.
      BF637.N4W66   1990   90-35559   CIP
      158'.5—dc20

Printed in the United States of America

1   2   3   4   5   6   7   8   9   10

This book is printed on acid-free paper.
                              ∞

To my family
To my wife, Anne, and my three wonderful children, Stacey, Gary, and Tiffany.

To the memories of my parents, Dr. Joseph and Anna R. Woolf, my in-laws, Abraham and Bertha Passman, my brother, Irving Woolf, and my friend Jerry Paris, actor and director extraordinaire.

Contents

11

Part Two
101 PROVEN TACTICS, TECHNIQUES, AND STRATEGIES

Foreword

LIKABILITY AND RESPECT. These are two qualities I've often found important in the daily goings and comings of life. If you can find it in someone who is also representing you, you are a fortunate person indeed. I've been very fortunate. Bob Woolf has represented me since 1978. We started somewhere around $50,000 a year. Thanks to Bob's negotiating talents, things are quite different now. But money is not the main factor with Bob Woolf. There are larger things. Things like integrity, truth, fairness, consideration, a friendly shoulder, an "always there" approach. Bob Woolf has all of these in spades. When I was given an advance copy of this book and was told it would be a "How to" kind of presentation, that is, Bob would share his secrets with readers, helping them *negotiate their way through life,* I thought, "How could this be?" I didn't think Bob Woolf had any method except being Bob Woolf, which was pretty good in and of itself. However, once you start to read, you learn there are many aspects to this seemingly innocent, yet multifaceted man. The fact that he is willing to share these concepts with readers is of good fortune to the reader. Bob Woolf does not need the money this book will no doubt make. He is therefore providing a public service. It is very hard to explain any method, especially when it comes so naturally to you, and in these pages Woolf successfully does just that. He is able to take sometimes complex negotiating situations, and break them down into everyday, workable, easy-to-follow concepts for any facet of life. You could use this book to determine what movie you're going to see tonight, especially if it's one your spouse doesn't want to see. On the other hand, you could also use it not only to get that raise you certainly deserve, but to get that extra weekend off. Maybe the company car. Maybe lots of other things you never thought of. When Bob Woolf represents you, you have a twenty-four-hour person. Anytime, day or night, seven days a week, Bob is reachable. This book can serve the same purpose for you.

On a personal note, when I went in for my heart surgery in late 1987, Bob was the first one at the hospital and the last one to leave. I was there eight days. He was there all eight days. He was a constant source of inspiration for my impending journey with the scalpel. A week after leaving the hospital, I spent two weeks recuperating at his lovely home in Florida with his terrific family. We shared a lot of life together during those two weeks, which only affirmed why Bob has become not only my representative, but also my confidant and friend. So, I may assure the reader on two counts. One, you're going to learn an awful lot that's going to help you an awful lot, and two, you're being helped along by an awfully terrific guy.

—LARRY KING

Acknowledgments

THE PREPARATION for this book spanned many years and was enhanced by the very helpful efforts of many fine, talented, and dedicated people. I am grateful to three excellent writers who helped me to bring my ideas to the written page: Richard Sandomir, Mickey Herskowitz, and Peter Knobler.

I would like to thank the President of the Putnam Berkley Group, Inc., Mrs. Phyllis Grann, for her never-ending support and enthusiasm for this book. And, of course, I should like to thank my Putnam editor, Ms. Stacy Creamer, whose outstanding professional experience and personal commitment helped me to organize my thoughts in a more concise manner for the readers.

I would like to acknowledge my book representative, Jay Acton, who ably guided me toward the reality of *Friendly Persuasion: My Life As a Negotiator.*

I would also like to thank my family, friends, and office staff for their input, patience, and interest in my writing endeavors.

ACKNOWLEDGMENTS

No amount of words can express my gratitude to my associate, Angelica Joan Francesca Leone, better known as Jill, who utilized her seventeen years' experience with my firm to help me articulate many of the experiences and nuances of negotiating expressed in this book. A very special thanks to her.

Part One

CHAPTER ONE

Friendly Persuasion: My Philosophy

"To be persuasive, we must be believable.
To be believable, we must be credible.
To be credible, we must be truthful."

—EDWARD R. MURROW

"Give to every other human being every right that you claim for
yourself."

—ROBERT G. INGERSOLL

THE PHONE rang at 7 P.M. in my Brookline, Massachusetts home. It
was the spring of 1985. "Bob," said the excited voice on the other end,
"you're a bleeping genius."

The caller was Donald Trump. He was exulting over the crush of
media coverage from his signing of Boston College quarterback Doug

Flutie to a six-year $8.3 million contract to play for Trump's United States Football League team, the New Jersey Generals.

My talks with Trump had been like a long ride on a gold-plated roller coaster. At one point, Trump had said he would pay anything for the charismatic Flutie, who stands only five-feet-nine, three-quarters inch; at another he pulled out of the negotiations completely, only to be goaded back to the table by our mutual friend, Howard Cosell.

The day before, we verbally agreed to the terms. But as I urged Trump into making the signing public, he backed off.

"If I do a hundred real estate deals, sixty will get signed," he said. "The other forty will get screwed up by the lawyers and never happen."

Knowing that he had pulled out before, I wanted Donald to make the announcement right away because it would provide greater insurance for my client that our agreement would really get signed. I promised him that this deal would go through. "I will make sure," I said, "that you are never embarrassed."

I needed to make Trump understand how good he would look by signing Flutie. He'd made big media splashes with the Grand Hyatt Hotel, Trump Tower, Trump Plaza, and his Atlantic City casinos. But I assured him, "If you go public with word of Flutie's signing, you will get more exposure this weekend than you have ever had in your life."

Finally persuaded, Trump made the announcement at 10 A.M. in the lobby of Trump Tower. The two-story waterfall in the building's atrium served as the backdrop for the conference. Reporters swarmed around the podium. Photographers' cameras flashed. That night, Trump was on the nightly news on all three networks. Newspapers headlined the story. The photos showed the handsome countenances of Trump and Flutie. Dan Rather introduced a clip on the evening news by calling the Flutie deal "the biggest contract in pro football history." My client was newly wealthy and Trump was thrilled to pay for the privilege of signing Doug.

So by the end of the day, Trump was calling me a genius—me, who had just cost him $8.3 million. I had done my job.

* * *

In October, 1988, I got a call from John Sasso, the campaign manager for Massachusetts Governor Michael Dukakis, then Democratic candidate for president. At the time, I was working as an advisor and fundraiser for Dukakis, an old friend and neighbor in Brookline, Massachusetts. The six kids we had between us had gone to the same public schools. I was only too happy to help my old friend in his attempt to get to the White House.

My main job was to convince team sports owners, entertainment executives and business moguls to donate $100,000 to the Democratic Victory Fund. With these wealthy people, I was negotiating access. These men were worth $400 million or more. I would simply say to them, "Would you rather keep all your $400 million or have $399,900,000, fly on the candidate's airplane, campaign with him and, if he's elected, have access to the President and be invited to the White House?" You'd be surprised how many wrote checks for $100,000 when it was put to them that way.

Sasso's call came a few days before Election Day. He was frantic. He said that Roone Arledge, the president of ABC News, had canceled a rare face-to-face "Nightline" interview between Dukakis and Ted Koppel because Michael had already agreed to be on Larry King's Cable News Network show earlier that evening.

Koppel felt King would steal his evening's newsmaking thunder and was insisting that Michael either reschedule his appearance on the King show or forgo the opportunity to appear on "Nightline." Dukakis didn't want to renege on his commitment to King. By the time Sasso reached me, the situation was grim.

"I'm in a panic, Bob," said Sasso. "It looks like we're going to lose 'Nightline.' Can you recover this for us? We need it badly."

"Let me try," I said. "Give me some time to think about it."

Sasso had said that Dukakis would fully honor his commitment to appear on King's show even if it meant losing the Koppel interview. My job was to find a way for Dukakis to be on *both*.

Here I was with the responsibility of reversing the loss of the "Nightline" plum, one of the most important forums in television, where

Michael could appear alone for ninety minutes. George Bush had said no to making a joint appearance. The ninety minutes of free air time was like winning the lottery. This was a chance to jump-start Dukakis's faltering candidacy during the most crucial phase of the campaign.

I called Roone in his New York office.

"I've got 100 reporters waiting outside my office for a decision," he said, "and at noon I'm going to announce that Ted won't do it."

"Why?" I asked.

"Ted's concerned that it'll steal his thunder," said Roone, who didn't agree with Koppel's thinking although he would support his ultimate decision. "But having Dukakis appear means a lot to Ted," he was equally quick to emphasize.

"Okay," I said, "please just give me some time to try to work something out before you go ahead with an announcement." He gave me an hour. In that time I needed to come up with something more agreeable to all parties and less threatening to Koppel.

That's when I decided I needed more information about the two programs. I called King's show and found out, to my delight, that not only was Michael scheduled to be on the show, but so was his wife, Kitty. Michael was to do thirty minutes alone, and eight together with Kitty. Kitty would do the final twenty-two minutes alone. That was the first I knew about the format, and it gave me options. I knew if Michael's time was reduced, it could help alleviate Koppel's concern as well as his objection.

Quickly, I called Roone. "Did you know that Michael isn't doing the whole King show, that Kitty is doing it, too?"

"No," said Roone, "I didn't know that."

"Larry's doing much more of a personality show than Ted will do," I said. "That won't be a threat to Ted's format and will lessen Ted's fears."

Roone agreed. "But we are running out of time," he warned.

Noon was approaching. My hour was almost up. I asked Roone for another hour.

"I'll do my best but I can't promise," he said. "But keep working on it." That gave me more time to maneuver. Arledge was leaving the door open. By extending the deadline, I felt he agreed that the King format wasn't that much of a threat to Koppel, and that Koppel could change his mind. But I still felt time closing in on me.

I called Sasso. He had Dukakis on the line. I put a call through to Roone. He had Koppel on one of his lines. I also had the producers of "Nightline" and King's show on two additional lines.

I went back and forth between the different lines, exploring various alternatives. Finally, we were able to hammer out an agreement whereby Michael would appear on King's show for twenty-two minutes, then for eight minutes together with Kitty. Kitty would do the remaining thirty minutes alone. The change, shifting eight minutes of air time from Michael to Kitty, wasn't huge, but it made enough of a difference to satisfy Koppel.

The agreement was announced at 1:30 P.M. to the anxious crowd of reporters assembled outside Arledge's office. Throughout the negotiations there was no screaming, no tantrums, just two sides trying to get what they wanted. Having Michael Dukakis appear on "Nightline" was almost as important for ABC News, as part of its coverage of the presidential campaign, as it was for the campaign itself. Arledge wouldn't have gone the extra mile with me if he didn't recognize the importance of the interview.

All parties walked away happy. I had done my job.

The grim call came to me late in the afternoon a few days before Thanksgiving Day of 1989. John Kent Cooke, son of the owner of the Washington Redskins, alerted me to the news that Dexter Manley, one of the greatest defensive ends in football history, had failed a drug test. This was the third time urinalysis had indicated there were drugs in Dexter's system. In the National Football League, three failures mean banishment from the game, a sentence that only the NFL Commissioner can revoke after a year's time.

Shortly after Cooke's call came another from the new commissioner, Paul Tagliabue. Would I bring Dexter to a meeting the next morning? This would be the first time I'd faced Tagliabue; Dexter's two previous suspensions had been imposed by former commissioner Pete Rozelle. In those suspensions, Dexter was required to undergo twice-weekly drug tests, and he failed one of them.

When I spoke to Dexter, he was in a state of shock, but more importantly, he was in a state of outright denial. Even though he had tested positive for drugs, he said the result was absolutely impossible. No, he insisted, he didn't use drugs. The test was wrong, not Dexter. He had unfailingly passed drug tests for eighteen months since the second suspension. He admitted that he had abused alcohol but said he never used drugs like cocaine. This *had* to be wrong.

Dexter's denials were heartbreaking. Like many addicts who relapse, he couldn't bring himself to admit his problem. Here was a young man who led an exemplary public life. He had stirringly admitted that he was illiterate and became a prominent spokesman for the literacy movement, testifying eloquently before Congress. Only two weeks before Cooke's call, Dexter and I sat in the home of Hollywood producer Leonard Goldberg when Goldberg had bought the rights to Dexter's inspiring life story, centered on his triumphant struggle to learn to read. Dexter had also worked diligently to tell kids to stay off drugs, kept a position with a local bank, and had his own radio and TV shows.

Now I had to persuade Dexter to admit that he was a drug addict and to tell his team and his fans that drugs had felled him. Dexter and I would have to take the first step, meeting with the commissioner, amid the glare of intense media scrutiny. Although our meeting with the commissioner was supposed to be private, the press knew about it. *The Washington Post* headlined it on its front page that day, and reporters surrounded us as we headed into Commissioner Tagliabue's office.

At our meeting, Tagliabue told me that Dexter had failed the drug test with a substantial amount of drugs in his system. Dexter again denied it, insisting the test was wrong, not him. He said he had tested negatively four days after the positive test and that it was impossible for the system to clear out so quickly.

I asked Commissioner Tagliabue to talk to doctors about whether

Dexter's system could be cleansed so rapidly, hoping that his research might give us a few days before he rendered his decision. I tried to make it clear that Dexter had been clean for a year and a half and that he wasn't a habitual abuser. He had erred once, and hadn't committed a crime while on drugs. He was a good person who had inexplicably slipped. I thought we had a reasonable case for leniency. Yet I knew that Tagliabue, previously the league's chief counsel, would have to handle Dexter's case according to league rules.

When we faced the press awaiting us, I cast our meeting in the best possible light. "I don't know what will happen," I said. "The commissioner is investigating the matter." I certainly couldn't admit anything about Dexter's drug problems if he wouldn't admit them to me or himself.

But the bad news came the next day, a Saturday: Tagliabue banned Dexter from the NFL for life. Dexter didn't take it well. He continued to deny using cocaine. He said he'd been railroaded, that he wouldn't accept banishment. People called him to tell him the action was race-related. He said we'd have to fight back. His family wanted him to sue. I urged him not to make public statements that would anger the commissioner or to listen to people filling his head with irrational schemes. His whole future depended on his conduct.

If Dexter would admit to using drugs, I hoped that Commissioner Tagliabue would be sympathetic enough to reinstate him as soon as possible. I prayed that Dexter wouldn't place himself in further jeopardy by making any ill-advised or ill-timed statements which could ruin his whole life. This was so traumatic for him and absolutely the wrong time for him to speak or act publicly. It was my job to speak and act for him until he was able to speak forthrightly about his addiction.

Sunday, Monday, and Tuesday went by. Dexter was still deeply into denial and anger. Our conversations sounded something like this:

"I'm not an addict."

"But why aren't you in the NFL?"

"I just slipped."

"You don't slip if you're not an addict."

Then on Wednesday, he called. He was crying. "I didn't tell you the truth, Mr. Woolf," he said. "I slipped. I took drugs." It's the first time he had admitted this to me, perhaps the first time he'd said it to anyone. Now I had to persuade him to say the same thing to his public. But when I told him that he must make the step, he said he was not ready for it.

Then providence seemed to intervene. Shortly after talking to Dexter, Houston Rockets guard John Lucas called me. He was in Boston to play the Celtics and asked me if he could help Dexter. Lucas was in a unique position to provide counsel: he had twice been banned from the National Basketball Association, but had rehabilitated from his drug addiction. Not only was he a productive, exciting player again, but even more significantly, he had also helped establish a drug rehabilitation clinic at a Houston hospital and was head of the National Basketball Players Association's drug committee.

"Only one addict can help another," Lucas told me.

So John came to my office from his Boston hotel room and called Dexter. I could tell from the way they were talking that John knew what Dexter was suffering through. Here was one recovering addict talking to a lapsed addict. Both were athletes of great accomplishment who had sacrificed all the good things in their lives because of drugs. John had come through it, and as I listened to him talking, his conversation seemed to me almost like a religious experience, as if God was trying to reach Dexter Manley through John Lucas.

Lucas pleaded with him, saying over and over, "You're an addict," and hoping that Dexter would relent. But Dexter, who had said that he'd slipped, still contended that he was not addicted to drugs.

After the Rockets–Celtics game that night, John and I talked to Dexter by telephone into the morning's wee hours, encouraging Dexter to come forward, to admit his problem and enter rehabilitation. I needed to help Dexter realize what his next step had to be. In many ways it was the toughest negotiation of my life. I was up against a very real psychological obstacle, Dexter's total fear of admitting that he was an addict who needed immediate help. I told Dexter that if he could come forward to help himself that he would still be able to salvage all the blessings he had in life—his family, his teammates, his football talents. I told him that he owed it to his loved ones and to the Redskins to do the right thing at this time. I told him that his courageous effort would be an incredible example to the world, that a person in the grips of a drug problem could recover and could regain every positive aspect of their life.

Finally, I told Dexter, "This is what I'm doing. I'm coming to Washington and we're having a press conference. You're going to be there. We'll work on a statement, and you won't say anything to the press but that statement. You'll admit that you used cocaine, and then you'll go straight to John Lucas's hospital for rehabilitation."

Dexter sounded undecided. Clearly, he couldn't seem to make that all-important admission, but yet it was obvious that he wanted to help himself. By suggesting a statement that would be as close as I felt he could get to making such an admission, I was trying to get him to take the next positive step. So I called a Saturday morning press conference, uncertain whether Dexter would even show up. I flew to Washington Friday night and spent the whole evening in my hotel room drafting the statement. Dexter did arrive and we met early the next morning before the press conference.

Dexter was pleased with the statement and felt it properly reflected the way he really felt. We rehearsed the statement together, both to familiarize Dexter with its contents and to prove to the press that Dexter, who came to pro football unable to read, was now indeed a literate man. I wanted the press and the public to know that Dexter was a man who was capable of recognizing a weakness and of working very hard to overcome that weakness, as I knew he would need the support of everyone around him to help him through his next personal battle.

Dexter stood up and read his statement to the press jammed into the room that morning. He began by saying that he'd made a "grave mistake by slipping up and using drugs. The tests were not wrong—*I was*. But I wouldn't admit it to anyone. I am sorry. Very sorry. I didn't stop to think about the debilitating effect it would have on my life and how it would hurt my career. Everything I'd achieved was destroyed by my senseless behavior. I underestimated the insidious nature of this disease."

I was as proud of Dexter as I have ever been of a client. It was

27

obviously a difficult and solemn moment in his life. He had faced his problem publicly and immediately left Washington for rehabilitation. Only by reestablishing his integrity and credibility could Dexter accomplish that goal. Dexter Manley had begun to walk that path. As some people said after the press conference, Dexter had done the "manly" thing. I had done my job.

What do these three stories have in common? They all involved a negotiation where money was not the main issue. When most people think of a negotiation they think in terms of money. Negotiations can involve ideas, decisions, philosophies, diplomacy, political viewpoints, and just as important, everyday interactions with others.

In the case of Donald Trump and Doug Flutie, my responsibility was convincing Trump that the favorable press exposure was worth making an immediate commitment. With the Ted Koppel and Governor Dukakis problem, it was mollifying Koppel's concerns about not having the first chance for an interview. In the case of Dexter Manley, the issue was not just attempting to save the career of a great football player, it was persuading Dexter to take control of his life.

In a negotiation, we are trying not only to sell an idea, but we are also trying to *persuade someone to adopt our viewpoint*, as pleasantly and accommodatingly as possible. We are trying to convince them to give us their money, their time, their services, that is, whatever *we* need, and to complicate matters even more, we want them to be happy about it.

The experience of negotiating with the likes of Donald Trump, Roone Arledge, and Commissioner Tagliabue and countless other executives and having negotiated over two thousand contracts for professional athletes alone prompted several publishers to ask me to write a book on the art of negotiating. As a result, I've really had to think hard and search my soul about what it is I do. For me, negotiating is very instinctive. My task as a writer was to translate these instincts into simple principles, a practical guide for people dealing with people, whether they were negotiating for a new multimillion-dollar contract for a prominent athlete or for a new kitchen in their own home. As I started to set down my thoughts, I realized that I had developed a way of negotiating and treating people that works well. For many years I didn't realize it. But as I thought back to how I started negotiating, I realized that I had been doing it since I was eight years old, growing up in Portland, Maine.

At that age, I delivered newspapers to my neighbors twice a day, in the morning and the afternoon. I earned a penny a paper. On my route, I learned some basic lessons: be reliable. Be prompt. Don't leave the paper in the snow or a puddle. By satisfying my customers' needs, my small route of twelve customers quickly grew to more than 100.

At age sixteen, after my family moved to Boston, I formed my own company, The Woolf Supply Company of New England. In a fourth-hand ramshackle jalopy, I was the middleman who bought various household items from the factory and sold them to local stores. I sold products ranging from A to Z—Anacin, Arrid, Alka-Seltzer, Band-Aids and Bromo Seltzer all the way to zinc ointment. I gave storeowners a fair deal. I was timely and delivered on my promises. I was able to make a profit and they had products on their shelves faster than they normally would have. Both sides were satisfied.

I graduated from Boston Latin School, and later from Boston College, where I was fortunate to have received a four-year basketball scholarship. From there, I went to Boston University Law School and, in 1952, successfully petitioned the Massachusetts Supreme Court to allow me to take the bar exam before I graduated. I passed the Massachusetts Bar before graduation from law school and, following a two-year stint in the Army, opened my own practice as a criminal defense attorney.

I was able to hone my negotiation skills as a litigator, learning how to persuade judges and juries that my viewpoint, expressed calmly and cogently, and without anger, was correct. I found myself able to gently impeach witnesses testifying against my clients and knew when my client could represent himself well as a witness, and when he could not. I won over 90 percent of my jury trials and had a successful practice, with eight attorneys working for me.

Then came the client who changed my life: Earl Wilson, a hard-throwing right-hander from the Boston Red Sox, came to me for help in 1964. Having recently pitched a no-hitter, he had been inundated with requests for personal appearances and endorsements. Since I was already helping Earl with his taxes and investments, he also asked me to help him with these numerous requests, which I did. He was kind enough to refer me to teammates like Carl Yastrzemski, Reggie Smith, George Scott, Ken Harrelson, and most of the Red Sox of the era.

Word spread in Boston. And suddenly, I heard from Boston Celtics players John Havlicek, Sam Jones, Bailey Howell, Wayne Embry, and Larry Siegfried. Soon I represented nine of the team's twelve players. Then came inquiries from several Boston Bruins, including Ted Green, Wayne Cashman, and Gerry Cheevers, and Boston Patriots like Gino Cappelletti, Houston Antwine, and Jimmy Lee Hunt.

I had assumed that most players were already represented, but to my surprise I found that most professional athletes had no legal or professional counsel. Those with agents were few and far between. As players for Boston franchises were traded to other teams, word spread around the country about my player representation. Players around the country began to ask me for my help. I was thrilled to represent a growing roster of sports stars and negotiate with successful and wealthy team owners.

Without planning it, I became the first sports attorney in the country. I get credit for being brilliant for having had the foresight to stake out this new frontier, but the truth is that I just happened to be in the right place at the right time.

From the beginning of professional sports, teams had treated their players very paternalistically. Maybe it was because the owners were men and the players started out as boys. Whatever the reason, there was definitely a "we'll take care of you" attitude on the part of team management. Unfortunately, that sentiment lasted only as long as the athlete's prowess. Then he was traded or tossed aside and another player took his place. With no competition for his services to use as leverage, and nowhere to go for an impartial hearing, an athlete's power was extremely limited. He could do nothing but what management wanted, and if he was turned down he could do nothing but accept a team's counteroffer or just not play. This system produced major frustrations and a climate for angry confrontations.

As a "friend of the family," I could present a player's case in a more reasoned, less emotional light than he could himself, and I could work with the club to take care of the kinds of problems that inevitably arose of which they wanted no part. I could get a player out of jail, help when outside influences like paternity suits or bankruptcy or automobile accidents might have disrupted a player's on-field concentration. I could take care of the player in ways the clubs had no interest in pursuing, and as a result, let the player produce for the club the way they wanted him to, the way they paid him to. I was accepted by the teams not out of their sympathy or understanding for the rights of an employee to be fairly represented; far from it. I was ultimately accepted because I worked with the clubs to everyone's mutual benefit.

After the 1966 season, when Wilson was traded to the Detroit Tigers, he asked me to help negotiate his contract. They wouldn't let me into the office to negotiate directly on his behalf. So I sat in Earl's apartment and every time he hit a rough spot in his talks with Tigers general manager Jim Campbell, he'd call me for guidance. Eventually, an agreement was signed.

Gradually, on other occasions, without trying to bash down the doors of the owners' sanctified men's clubs—where representatives feared to tread—I was able to gain the team's confidence that I would negotiate fairly. The door was opening. Within five years, I had 300 clients in all sports and in nearly all major league cities. At the same time, I hopefully acquired a reputation for dealing with my opponents fairly.

Without realizing it, I was a pioneer in a new industry. My own business grew faster than I could have dreamed. For me, representing star players like Carl Yastrzemski, Jim Plunkett, John Havlicek, Julius Erving, and Ken Harrelson in the early days and Larry Bird, Joe Montana, Vinny Testaverde, Byron Scott, and Doug Flutie today has meant the fulfillment of Walter Mitty-esque fantasies.

It's been enormously satisfying to advise and guide some of the top athletes in the world, and it's been equally satisfying to negotiate across the table with Ted Turner, Sonny Werblin, Pete Rozelle, Bowie Kuhn, Bill Veeck, Tom Yawkey, Joe Robbie, shopping mall magnate Ed DeBartolo Jr., all four network presidents, the owners of most major-market TV stations, the heads of the leading advertising agencies and top executives of Fortune 500 companies.

They are all people of considerable wealth and will, leaders in their industries, and expert judges of sports, entertainment, and business talent.

By the early 1970s I had developed an expertise in representing sports figures. It wasn't long before I started hearing from TV and radio personalities, actors and actresses, choreographers, directors, producers, screenwriters, and authors. Like athletes, they had a creative talent and a market value. They needed to have their contracts professionally negotiated.

Today, the cross-section of clients I represent has expanded to an even greater variety. It's as wide-ranging as being counsel to the greatest violinist in the world, Itzhak Perlman, to the professional wrestler, George "The Animal" Steele; from Joan Kennedy to Meadowlark Lemon of the Harlem Globetrotters; from the former CIA Director Admiral Stansfield Turner to Dr. Robert Filler, the Toronto surgeon who separated Siamese twins; from Susan Butcher, four-time winner of the Iditarod dog race in Alaska, to Camelia Sadat, daughter of Anwar Sadat, the late president of Egypt; and from freed American hostage Frank Reed to the skyrocketing recording stars, the New Kids on the Block.

Over the years, because some of my clients were making bad investments, were prey to get-rich-quick schemes, weren't paying their taxes, were spending money unreasonably and getting into myriad financial problems, my work has gone far beyond negotiating contracts and has expanded to being their business and career manager as well.

In most cases, my clients' paychecks come directly to my office. They receive a mutually agreed-upon weekly allowance. All their bills are paid from the office. Their wills, trusts, corporate structures, insurance programs, and taxes are prepared for them and they are aided in planning their entire investment programs. In addition, we also negotiate their commercials, product endorsements, autobiographies, films, and television and personal appearances; anything that happens in their professional lives.

Since I am heavily involved in their professional lives, I also play a part in their personal lives. I advise many of my clients on issues from buying a car, a house or a plane to planning prenuptial agreements before they marry and negotiating settlements in the advent of divorce.

Handling millions of dollars annually, all sorts of business opportunities have been presented to me, from the suspect to the ridiculous to the legitimate. The range of investments that come a celebrity's way is incredible, and I've been involved in negotiations relating to stocks and bonds; cattle feeding and breeding; oil and gas exploration; syndicated real estate; railroad cars; tuna fish boats; mink farms; art work; movie deals; airplanes; oil rigs; container ships; shopping centers; warehouses; commercial buildings and garden apartments.

In reviewing my experiences over the years, I have followed a three-part philosophy for dealing with people that has been a constant throughout every one of my negotiations. I realize that these are the kind of precepts that most people take for granted, but they have become one of my most important negotiating tools. I do believe that these precepts, combined with the practical techniques that I will be showing you in this book, will lead you to consistently more successful negotiations and will allow you to be able to recognize and avoid the many pitfalls that can often destroy any negotiation. They are simple but effective guidelines applicable not only in negotiating but in dealing with people in everyday life: tenet number one, *You Don't Have to Be Disagreeable to Disagree*; number two, *The Golden Rule*, which is timeless; and number three, *Be True to Your Convictions*.

Following this philosophy makes my job easier and produces successful results, both for those I do business with and for me. I know they work because I've used them in the real world of negotiation, where being a practitioner, not a theorist, is what works. Taken together, the philosophy adds up to a method of treating people with fairness and respect. Believe it or not, that is the best way to negotiate.

You Don't Have To Be Disagreeable to Disagree

I have spoken to countless negotiators who practice their craft every day. And they agree with me, that any experienced negotiator can count on one hand the number of times a negotiation has descended into outright screaming and hostility.

I just think of some of the best negotiators I know, who are all tough and effective as well as fair, but who remain at all times cool and cordial in conducting their affairs. They get what they want, but they're not disagreeable in the process of getting it.

There are few negotiators with as long and successful a career as Thomas P. "Tip" O'Neill, the former speaker of the U.S. House of Representatives. He was a master at forming a consensus among his Democratic and Republican colleagues, employing a decidedly nonintimidating style that kept him from making enemies even when people didn't fully agree with him. His sociable approach to forging agreements between two very partisan factions allowed him to leave Capitol Hill beloved by those on both sides of the aisle.

Consider Armand Hammer, the ninety-two-year-old philanthropist, unofficial peace ambassador to the world, and chairman and chief executive officer of Occidental Petroleum. For nearly six decades, during some of the most strained times in relations between the United States and the Soviet Union, Hammer has been able to do business with the Soviets. Armand Hammer was the pioneer in United States–Soviet trade. He was conducting his personal *glasnost* with the Soviets as early as the 1930s by establishing a relationship of trust, by dealing with them in a straightforward manner, and by showing the Soviets how he could help them at the same time that he was helping himself. Do you think he accomplished this by ranting and raving and trying to intimidate the Russians? Do you think he was successful by being disagreeable? I would doubt it.

Then there's Pete Rozelle, the former commissioner of the National Football League. The quiet, ex-public relations man for the Los Angeles

Rams was elected commissioner by the owners in 1960. For over thirty years in that position, he retained the unqualified respect of the NFL owners while guiding the sport through new leagues and a variety of changes. Successfully maintaining a positive rapport over a thirty-year period with twenty-eight domineering personalities in the form of the NFL owners, who in the past have had problems even agreeing on matters as trivial as when to adjourn a meeting, is a tremendous testimonial to Pete Rozelle, and to a style of negotiating formed by respect, trust, even temperament, and diplomacy.

None of these men had to resort to ploys, deceptions, double-dealing, or underhanded methods to be successful. They did it the right way. Countless others do it the right way. And believe me, you can be a good, smart, tough, and effective negotiator and still do it the right way, too.

I'm aware of the many books with clever and tricky titles that want you to believe that the only way to succeed is to be intimidating and devious, often at the risk of your own ethics and integrity. Some of these books suggest methods which are directly contradictory to the basic natures of most people. These books perpetuate the misconception that negotiating is an underhanded, immoral, tricky, deceitful process. This is not so. In fact, people who use these methods usually find that their approach comes back to haunt them.

You have also probably heard a lot about winning through intimidation. Many people believe that you have to be intimidating, forceful, even rude to be a successful negotiator. This is another misconception and everywhere I go, I face it head on. People approach me in airports, restaurants, and the streets of Boston to offer congratulations on winning a big contract for a client, as if I'd KO'd Mike Tyson in ninety seconds. "You really gave it to him, Bob!" they say, revealing their inaccurate perspectives. I only nod politely in response. Inside, I'm amused.

I'm going to tell you the real truth about negotiating. It is not about going to war. It is about talking, not screaming. Negotiation is the respectable art of persuasion between two parties, whether the person on the other side of the table is Henry Kissinger or your local used-car salesman.

Another misconception is that in all negotiations there must be a winner and loser. That's a big mistake. The question should never be "Who won?" but "Was everybody satisfied?" I never think of negotiating *against* anyone, I work *with* people to come to an *agreement*. Both sides have a stake in making a deal come out right. It is important to make the other side understand that if I succeed they succeed, and vice versa.

In creating an atmosphere of good will, it is crucial to establish that negotiations are not win-or-lose situations but that both sides stand to gain. I make every effort to create *win-win* situations from the outset. This is a vital point. In fact, I prefer to call the person on the other side of the table my "bargaining or negotiating partner," rather than my adversary. I always like to begin with the understanding that my bargaining partner and I are working in concert to arrive at a condition that is mutually beneficial. Deals are put *together*. And it can all be done without being disagreeable.

The Golden Rule

The Golden Rule is one of the oldest and most revered guidelines to treating people fairly. It has never gone out of style. It's been true for 2,500 years, it'll be true for another 2,500 years. It is as pertinent in negotiations as it is in your dealings with relatives and loved ones. If you mistreat your adversary, don't expect him to show kindness toward you. That's a recipe for a failed negotiation.

I think Dale Carnegie expressed it best when he wrote, "Philosophers have been speculating on the rules of human relationships for thousands of years, and out of all that speculation, there has evolved only one important precept. It is not new. It is as old as history."

Zoroaster taught it to his followers in Persia twenty-five hundred years ago. Confucius preached it in China twenty-four centuries ago.

Lao-Tzu, the founder of Taoism, taught it to his disciples in the Valley of the Han. Buddha preached it on the banks of the holy Ganges five hundred years before Christ. The sacred books of Hinduism taught it a thousand years before that.

"Jesus taught it among the stony hills of Judea nineteen centuries ago. Jesus summed it up in one thought—probably the most important rule in the world: 'Do unto others as you would have others do unto you.' "

And when do you do it? All the time. I believe that if you treat people right, they will treat you right. People know if you treat them well and they know if you mistreat them. People aren't stupid. Even a dog knows the difference between being deliberately kicked and accidentally stepped on.

Through my experiences, I've dealt with the honest and the dishonest, the decent and the unscrupulous, the truthful and those who lie. So I'm not pretending to be a Pollyanna. I'm aware that people will tell you it's a cruel world out there. In some ways, it is. Yet I still hang onto these principles not only because I believe they are good and moral, but because they work. I know that the other side won't always treat me as I treat them. But I go into every negotiation expecting to be dealt with fairly. Almost always I am.

Franklin Delano Roosevelt believed in this simple principle of human relations. Said FDR, "If you treat people right, they'll treat you right—at least 90 percent of the time." I can live with those percentages. If you follow the path set forth in this book, you'll be able to handle the other 10 percent.

Be True to Your Convictions

The third cornerstone to my philosophy is to stick to what you believe in: your convictions, values, and standards. For your own self-esteem and for the respect you hope to earn from others, you can't change your beliefs to fit each new situation and fashion. Making your ethics subject to a whim is a prescription for mistrust. Almost certainly your negotiations will be doomed to failure.

Nothing better illustrates my belief in standing by your convictions than the talks that led up to my selection as Larry Bird's representative. Halfway through his final season at Indiana State University, Larry was touted as the finest college basketball player in the game. I began to hear from several NBA scouts that he might be the best they had ever seen. That caught my attention.

Boston Celtics president Red Auerbach had drafted Larry for the Celtics the year before his original college class graduated. Larry had spent part of a year at Indiana University, suffered an acute case of homesickness and dropped out for what would have been his freshman season. Drafting Bird as a junior was characteristically savvy of Red, whose shrewdness had built the Celtics dynasty.

Since Larry did not want the distraction of meeting with potential representatives, at his request, a committee of prominent townspeople in Terre Haute was formed to screen the hundreds of applicants.

The committee included Bob King, the Indiana State athletic director; Lucien Meis, the owner of the leading department store; the president of the local bank and an array of other top businessmen in town. It was impressive to see neighbors protect one of their own. They did not want to see Larry exploited.

There were sixty-five prospective agents on the original list. I don't know how many were interviewed, but I was delighted to be one of them. Landing in Terre Haute, I was driven directly from the airport to the country club, where the committee had reserved a meeting room. I sat at the head of a long conference table while everybody else sat on either side. They questioned me for eight hours on every pertinent subject. What would be an appropriate salary? How much, if any, should be deferred? Would there be a signing bonus? What would be the effect of inflation on a long-term contract? What were the tax consequences? How did I judge Larry's prospects for earnings outside his playing contract? What kind of investment opportunities should he expect? Endorsements? Personal appearances? Money management?

That night, I joined the group at the field house to watch Bird in action for the first time. I would not meet him on this trip.

I had begun to establish a rapport with several of the committee members, which I consider essential on virtually every level of negotiating. I am nearly always on the side of the seller: we have the product, or the service, that a specific buyer wants. This time there was a difference: I had to sell myself. In itself, this was not unusual. But dealing with a panel like this was. In no way did I resent the interview. I regarded it not as an audition, but as a chance to demonstrate my knowledge and my way of conducting business. And as much as they were looking to assess my ability to perform, I was watching these men for clues and hints as to Larry Bird's character.

I now knew the story behind his hasty exit from Indiana University, fifty miles from his home. He had enrolled at seventeen. It was not coach Bobby Knight who drove him away, it was his age and insecurity. His roommate had a closet filled with clothes. Bird had a change of blue jeans and one pair of shoes. "I was a homesick kid who was lost and broke," he would explain later. "If I knew then what I know now, I'd have run right back. Coach Knight and I would have had no trouble. He'd have loved my game."

Over the next few months, I would get a call from someone on the committee seeking advice on a specific question. Should Larry be insured? Should he play in postseason all-star games? Would his value be hurt by Indiana State's loss to Michigan in the NCAA championship finals? I gave them my opinions: yes, yes, no.

The committee cut the field of prospective representatives to twenty-five, then to fifteen. Eventually, I was called to be told I was one of three still being considered. The Cinderella season of Indiana State had just ended. It was now time to bring Bird into the decision-making process. This time the discussion would be more tightly focused, the dollars involved more specific.

I returned to Terre Haute for the second round. They took me to the same country club meeting room and we sat around the same table. But this time, Bird was there. I sat at one end. Larry sat at the other. Larry was dressed in overalls and sneakers and when we were introduced, he shook hands without saying a word. Even though Larry had already developed a reputation for being shy and a master of understatement, I still felt a little uneasy and off stride. I knew he had not talked to the press in school. But I was not a reporter.

Bird's distance from the press had been self-imposed. He was troubled by the attention he was receiving, which he felt was at the expense of his teammates. He thought if he refused to give interviews or attend press conferences, the media would seek out the other players and would have to write about them.

He finally ended his silence after thirty-three games, at a press conference the day before the finals. One of the first questions had to do with an injury to his thumb. He had played with it in a bandage most of the year.

"How's your thumb?" a reporter asked.

"Broke," he answered. Then he waited for the next question. That was all it meant to him.

So as I sat down at the conference table, I wondered about his personality: how difficult he might be, how articulate. The answers were not long in coming.

The members of the committee were eager to get into the area of salaries. Even the most professional among us has a curiosity about what other people earn. The nature of my business makes it crucial that I have access to these figures. I walked into that room with the numbers on virtually every contract of every top athlete in America.

By taking him a year early, the Celtics had already established that Bird was the top prospect in the draft, so I began by quoting figures for players of his status, with a special emphasis on Boston. I told the committee what Red Sox stars Jim Rice and Fred Lynn were making. You could feel the energy in the room rising.

Suddenly, one of the panel members interrupted. "How much does Tommy John make?" he asked. The Yankees' pitcher was from Terre Haute, and, until Larry came along, was the city's most famous citizen and the biggest sports star any of them had known. Excitedly, the cry went up around the table, "Yeah, how much does Tommy John make?"

Before I could shuffle my papers, Larry Bird, who had not said two words until then, broke in and said in a firm and clear voice, "Mr. Woolf, Tommy John happens to be a friend of mine." All conversations stopped. "I don't particularly care to know what he makes . . . or have anyone else know what he makes."

The natural instincts and sensitivity of this twenty-two-year-old impressed me powerfully. Those were the first words he ever really said to me and in one sentence he revealed his great character and integrity.

I was surprised and pleased when Bird drove me back to my room at the Holiday Inn. In the car, I told him that I admired his loyalty to Tommy John and his sense of decency. He responded with a shrug, but he talked easily the rest of the ride and I felt we had made genuine contact. I was almost certain I would get Larry as a client.

Back in my room, I called home to tell my wife, Anne, about the meeting, the remarkable maturity Larry had shown and how confident I felt about the prospect of representing him. My entire family was happy for me. We were all Boston fans and sensed that Larry Bird was going to be very special for Boston.

I had no sooner hung up and propped myself on the bed, when the phone rang. "Bob, this is Lucien Meis," the voice said. He was the department store owner on the committee. "Larry and some of us would like to come over to the motel and chat with you again." I couldn't tell whether this was good news or trouble and during the time it took them to reach my room I began to feel extremely anxious.

When the group arrived, Meis was the spokesman. "Look, Bob, this is the situation," he said. "The selection has been narrowed down to you and Reuven Katz (a highly respected attorney in Cincinnati who represents Pete Rose and Johnny Bench). We have got to know from you exactly what you are going to charge as your fee for representing Larry. Will it be $10,000? $40,000? Give us a dollar figure. We have got to know exactly what it is. Mr. Katz has given us a figure and we need one from you."

I felt my stomach tighten. The question had come up before. When they pressed, I had resisted answering. There was no way I could even approximate a figure that far in advance. I had no idea how long the negotiation would take or what the actual work would involve. I had explained to the committee that I did not work on a flat-fee basis. I have always worked on a percentage, with a maximum fee of 5 percent of the client's annual salary. The fairness of this practice has been upheld time and again over the years. This was the working relationship I had established with all my clients.

"Look," I said, addressing Meis, "I understand why you're asking me and I respect Larry's desire to know how much it will cost him. But I want to work with Larry the same way I have worked with everyone else. At the end of the negotiations when Larry has a contract, then we will agree upon a fee. I cannot give you a figure now. It wouldn't be fair to my other clients if I was to make a special adjustment in order to work with Larry. I want to represent him very much. I consider this a special opportunity. But I just can't give you the answer you want."

Meis stared at me. "Well, look, we just want to be sure that you understand the consequences," he said. The consequences, of course, were that I would not get Larry Bird as my client. Meis continued, "We're asking you again, give us a set figure and we can wrap this up. Chances are, I've got to tell you, that without it you will not be representing Larry Bird. Please give us a figure." Bird was sitting there, watching.

Quickly, I tried to calculate the possibilities. In Boston, where I lived, Larry Bird was already being canonized and his potential was unlimited. But if I compromised my basic way of working with him, then I shortchanged every one of my clients.

I took a deep breath, "I can't give you a figure," I said. "I can only repeat that my fee will be reasonable and I will work hard on Larry's behalf. But I will not treat Larry Bird any differently than anyone else I represent and I am prepared to accept the consequences." We all shook hands and they walked out of the room.

You can only stand and look at a door for so long. I felt righteous but miserable. I called home again and told Anne, "You won't believe what just happened." But she did, even the part about my apparently losing Bird as a client. My son, Gary, then a teenager, picked up the extension phone and said, "It's all right, Dad, I'm proud of you. You still have your principles and I'm glad that's what you did."

The principles might strike some as slightly fuzzy, but you cannot tailor your standards to fit that day's opportunity. It appeared that I had kept my principles, but at the cost of some substantial figure earnings and prestige. It sounds mighty noble to talk about putting honor above profit, but as clear a choice as that is supposed to be, in the real workplace it isn't.

Five minutes later, the phone rang.

"Bob, this is Lu Meis. I just wanted to tell you we've made our decision. We thought we shouldn't wait until morning to let you know."

"Yes?" I felt weary and drained and not very talkative. I braced for the bad news.

"We've decided on you."

I was shocked . . . and thrilled. "You're kidding!"

"No, Bob," Meis said. "We know how much you want to represent Larry, how much it means to you and how much time and effort you put into coming here. We decided that if you would stand up to us the way you did, stick to a position and just walk away, you are the kind of man we want negotiating for Larry against Red Auerbach."

Their decision made for a very pleasant flight back to Boston.

In a world where the only true constant is change, I'd like to hope that my philosophy stays unchanged. Now, with these principles as the guideposts, I'm going to take you on a tour of the stages of becoming a fair and successful negotiator. In the following pages, I will outline the steps, which include: developing a positive attitude, creating the right atmosphere, determining your needs, building a reputation, preparing your case, assessing and utilizing leverage, developing a style, putting yourself in the other person's shoes so you understand their motivations, and creating strategies and techniques to employ in every negotiation.

I will show you how to follow the same common-sense steps that I follow in negotiating seven-figure contracts for celebrities. These steps will help you with situations that you, your family, and friends encounter every day. These steps apply whether you are dealing with a corporate executive or a K-Mart store manager, and whether you're trying to get a raise or acquire a company.

The techniques that work for me will work for you because at their core, most negotiations are similar. It doesn't matter if the dollar figure is $50.00, $1,000.00 or a million dollars. It doesn't matter if you are dealing with your neighbor or heads of governments. The central difference between my working out a contract for a client and your getting a raise or promotion is experience. If you become a deft negotiator at the everyday level, you will have increasing success at a more complex level.

Just as a doctor prescribes preventive maintenance for your health, I will also be recommending preventive medicine for your negotiations. If you follow my prescription, you will be well-prepared to avoid some of the pitfalls of negotiation.

Once you've developed and used the techniques I've laid out, negotiations will be less threatening. As you continue to negotiate your day-to-day affairs, the process will become second nature to you. I'm not saying you will win every single negotiation. But the principles should lead to the kind of successful average that would please any business person. If you practice these simple principles, I guarantee you will become a dignified negotiator, one who is good, tough, smart, and effective. In short, you will become a better negotiator, one who more often than not gets what he or she wants.

CHAPTER TWO

Attitude and Atmosphere

"If you're not fired with enthusiasm, you will be fired with enthusiasm."

— VINCE LOMBARDI

"Be kind to people on the way up, because you're gonna meet them on the way down."

— ED NORTON, describing to RALPH KRAMDEN the amicable atmosphere he fosters in the N.Y.C. sewer system.

"There is very little difference in people, but that little difference makes a big difference. The little difference is attitude. The big difference is whether it is positive or negative."

— CLEMENT STONE

IN ORDER to start the process of making you a better negotiator, it's probably important to discuss just what is a negotiation. Very simply, to me, a negotiation is a transaction where you want something and somebody else wants something. A negotiation determines how much each side gets of what it wants.

Negotiation is the art of the possible, a road filled with detours called compromises. Your goal as a negotiator is to compromise as little as you can to get as much as possible. You can never expect to get *everything* you want. Your job as a negotiator is to persuade the other side to do what you would like them to do without forcing or demanding it.

The first thing you want to do is get the other side to understand what you want. You want them to see the matter from your point of view, to persuade them that your view is reasonable.

Nearly every successful negotiation can be boiled down to two sides giving and taking, making concessions and emerging, generally, with something close to what each party wants. It is an imperfect process, but there are no scientific ways to measure human persuasion.

Negotiating Is an Everyday Occurrence

I am always negotiating and so are you.

By the time I leave my house in the morning, I've already completed a host of negotiations. The kind of negotiations I'm talking about here aren't part of my business; they're part of my everyday life and probably yours. For example, on an average morning I'll negotiate with my wife about where we'll go for dinner that night or with my daughter about borrowing the family car. I'm sure you're involved in comparable negotiations every day of the week. We may not consciously think of these interpersonal dealings as negotiations, but that's what they are.

Think of all the small, unacknowledged negotiations you engage in every day. You drop clothes off at the dry cleaners. How soon will they be ready? You and a friend decide on a place for lunch. Is it uptown or downtown, at noon or at one? At night you agree to let your kids stay up for one more TV program, but then it's time for bed.

We tend to think of dealings as negotiations only when the stakes are high: how much will that renovation cost? In what religion will your children be raised? If you take that new job, what will the total compensation package be? The stakes may be higher, but the dynamics involved in negotiating the terms remain the same. The sooner you start realizing your dealings—be they personal or professional—as negotiations, the more adept a negotiator you'll be.

Don't Be Afraid of the Process

Most people fear the very idea of negotiating, expecting it to be something along the order of a root canal: a painful procedure as mystifying as it is costly. They fear the anticipated fallout: hurt feelings, ill will. People are reluctant to negotiate because they are afraid they will seem impolite, pushy, unfair, and maybe even cheap. Even when they are asking for something they feel is justified and fair, many people are reluctant to insist.

People also feel that if they take issue with someone else's position, they will be viewed as questioning that person's credibility or judgment. There is also the fear of getting caught up in a battle of wills or wits. People wonder if they will be outmatched or outclassed by their adversary.

I understand those fears. They are natural. Every negotiator experiences them. I have found that more often than not, your opponent feels exactly the same way you do. In that respect, the fear of the process is almost a common bond. You would both rather make it a pleasant experience rather than an unpleasant experience. But, if you follow the simple steps I suggest, you will be able to cope with even the most rattling situations if they arise.

I've always felt that rather than fear the person you're trying to

47

negotiate with, you should try to make him or her your partner. Your ally. Show patience and respect. Put them at ease. You don't want a negotiation to turn into a battle.

The Right Attitude

When I enter a negotiation, my attitude is, "I'm going to make a deal." I'm optimistic by nature. I don't start with a negative thought or word. I try to foster a spirit of cooperation. I want the other person to feel that I am forthright, cheerful, confident, and determined to reach a fair agreement.

When you're upbeat and positive, people will respond to you in kind. And when you're in the right frame of mind, you're more likely to feel you're going to reach your goal. To a degree, your attitude can become a self-fulfilling prophecy. If I'm sufficiently sensitive to the other person, I firmly believe that he'll be predisposed to making an agreement with me. If I'm positive, I'll be more readily accepted, and the other side is more likely to have a positive view of me.

Name a successful person in any profession and you're likely to find a positive attitude at work. Dr. Norman Vincent Peale has built a mini-empire predicated on "the power of positive thinking." Peale maintains that people have the power within themselves to succeed. I agree with him.

The right attitude has been demonstrated to be effective even in battling physical ailments. When Norman Cousins, the famous writer and editor, suffered a heart attack, he went on a campaign to be positive and happy, going so far as to watch old Marx Brothers movies in his hospital room. He believed he created a positive energy that proved crucial to his recovery.

Have you ever seen a Fuller Brush or Mary Kay Cosmetics salesperson on their door-to-door rounds? They go forward each day, carrying their wares, ringing doorbells and risking rejection at every turn. But to succeed and reap the rewards they can obtain, they charge ahead full of determination. Anyone who succeeds in sales knows that the right attitude is their most valuable asset.

A friend of mine, a door-to-door salesman, had the worst kind of luck. Day after day he'd walk up and down the streets with his product. No one would buy a thing. Every day he knocked on the same woman's door. Every day she turned him away. Finally he appeared on her doorstep for the umpteenth time. Just to keep the man from ever returning, the woman made a purchase. The next day, my friend rang her doorbell again. "What are you doing here?" she asked, exasperated.

My friend replied, "Well, now that you're an established customer . . ."

How's that for a positive attitude?

Remember, a good attitude can be as contagious as laughter. Spread cheer, not jeer.

The Importance of Creating a Good Atmosphere

Doesn't everyone want to make a good impression to win over an employer, a client or a friend? Sure. We want to create an atmosphere where people will be receptive to us.

That's why corporations spend billions of dollars on advertising and public relations campaigns to sell their products and nurture a buyer's positive attitude toward them.

Before a sale is made, the initial marketing efforts are designed to create an atmosphere of trust and respect in people and arouse in them a desire to buy what is being sold. Companies want to show they treat their customers properly and they make a good product or perform a valuable service. They want to show they're a good corporate citizen. That's exactly what I want to do when I negotiate; create the right atmosphere for an agreement to be reached. I want the other person sold on me and my product. I want people to be receptive to me. I want them to trust and respect me and to feel that I am a person with integrity.

Once you have become aware of creating an atmosphere as a negotiation strategy, you will be surprised to learn how many people utilize it. I saw this on vivid display during my first meeting with Donald Trump before negotiations began to sign Doug Flutie to a contract to play for Donald's United States Football League entry, the New Jersey Generals.

By this time—1985—Trump had built quite a reputation for himself. He was flamboyant, aggressive, and unpredictable as well as a fabulously wealthy and successful businessman. I didn't quite know which famed Trump to expect: the shrewd developer, the egocentric sportsman, the generous philanthropist, or the would-be politician.

Trump was preceded by his reputation for being charismatic, slightly arrogant, and intimidating. He had developed the $40 million real estate company his father had left him into a multibillion-dollar empire with massive holdings in midtown Manhattan. And he put his name on everything. Trump Tower was his most impressive accomplishment, an aggressively architectured building complex on Fifth Avenue which included a flashy array of designer boutiques topped by some of the most expensive condominiums in the city.

Trump's offices were in Trump Tower. Entering the building through glass doors opened by gracious and immaculately uniformed doormen, one is immediately struck by the grand scale of the vast and busy arcade. Three stories high, it is graced with polished red marble floors, gold railings, and a series of silent escalators taking posh shoppers to the next level of the latest in fashion. A two-story indoor waterfall laps along one long wall, soothing the well-dressed clientele of the Tower's open-air café.

Trump has a private elevator which brings to him his guests and business acquaintances, but you have to state your business to the two men who guard it before being escorted to the twenty-sixth floor.

Doug and I were accompanied by Doug's father, Dick, and Gerard Phelan, who had caught Doug's "miracle" pass only months before. We were greeted by Trump's receptionist, who said that Mr. Trump was expecting us. After a few moments Trump himself appeared. We shook hands and he said, "I am running a few minutes late. Please excuse me. Perhaps you would like to step inside and see a short film I have made."

Trump ushered us into a small, private screening room which seated about twenty. We were the only people there. Trump excused himself and left. The lights went down and the curtains parted and for the next twenty minutes we were shown a slickly produced, visually attractive, highly impressive presentation detailing the triumphs and achievements of Donald Trump. It was impressive. It was his commercial. Maybe he wanted to make sure we knew the extent of his accomplishments. It was his attempt to earn our respect and create the right atmosphere before our negotiations took place. Only after we had seen the film in its entirety were we shown into Mr. Trump's office.

Power and influence hung in the air like cologne. A scale model of "Television City," Trump's latest project involving roughly seventy-five acres of Manhattan's Upper West Side along the Hudson River with plans to develop the entire area plus erect the world's tallest building, was spread across a table like the future.

And the vista was fabulous. From the room-length windows you received a panorama of New York City—it was all displayed before us, a beautiful and expansive sight. The World Trade Center, lower Manhattan, Greenwich Village, Chelsea, the Empire State Building, the glass and steel towers of midtown, Central Park, and beyond. Trump took the young football star over to the window for a closer view.

"There's ABC, NBC, CBS," he said, motioning to the surrounding skyscrapers that housed the three networks. "The city is at your beck and call. This is your city, Doug," he confided. "It's at your feet."

I thought we'd be heading downstairs for lunch at a fancy place like "21," but Trump had something else in store: he sent out for sandwiches. A bag lunch with a billionaire. It wasn't a bad touch. He had tried to temper a potentially intimidating situation by showing us he was a regular guy.

But basically he was looking to gain our respect. I can't blame him for doing this. Trump is a good negotiator.

The late Malcolm Forbes, publisher of *Forbes* magazine, went to comparable lengths to put his negotiating partners at ease. Forbes frequently invited major corporate CEOs to lunch with him in the magazine's private dining room. Intimate one-on-one lunches often transpired downstairs in the cozy comfort of Forbes's wine cellar.

Forbes also used his yacht, *The Highlander*, as a sociable business setting. Each year, he invited twenty-five CEOs at a time for six outings to cruise up the Hudson River with the Forbes family. Forbes said he liked to see the CEOs relax and mingle with their peers.

Why did Forbes make this effort? He knew that you can't run a business, much less a magazine, through intimidating tactics and corporate fiat alone. By getting to know these executives and allowing them the chance to get to know him, he ensured the right kind of friendly, personable atmosphere for future negotiations. Forbes wanted to sell advertising for his magazine and create access for his editors and writers to the CEOs and their companies. Entertaining them could only enhance his position for either endeavor. Malcolm Forbes was a good negotiator.

When I talk about creating the right atmosphere, I am referring to the attitude that both parties bring to the table, whether it be at a train station, a fast-food restaurant, or a five-star restaurant. While it may be pleasant to negotiate in a lavish hotel or a French restaurant, the proper atmosphere is not physical. It is a state of mind, a friendly and open climate where the right impressions are created ahead of time, where you've put yourself in the best light even before sitting down to talks, and where both sides have trust and respect for each other. If you have the right attitude, you can negotiate anywhere. While you can't control your negotiating partner's thinking, the way you approach him, the kind of overtures you make, can influence it.

I once negotiated a contract on behalf of Sidney Green, with Jonathon Kovler, then co-owner of the Chicago Bulls, while floating atop rubber rafts on Horse Pond near my home on Cape Cod. I'll do everything in my power to create the kind of atmosphere where my negotiating partner enters the talks with an attitude favorable to making a deal. If he already trusts me, it will make my job easier.

Whenever I'm in doubt that someone doesn't have the proper attitude toward me or doesn't know my credentials, I'll try to have someone call on my behalf. Or I'll call in advance to show my attitude, that I'm looking forward to our meeting and encouraging them that we will make a deal.

When these avenues of communication are closed to me, I have to depend on their knowledge of my reputation for integrity, keeping my word and ethics. You work a whole lifetime to build a reputation which you hope will benefit you when it precedes you.

Building Your Reputation

The value of a good reputation can't be overemphasized. When I negotiate with somebody who is familiar with me, I know I don't need to start establishing a reputation. They already know the kind of person with whom they are dealing.

To me, a reputation is the sum total of how you have conducted yourself in your professional and personal affairs. If you have shown respect, integrity, and character in all your dealings, people have a tendency to know about it. Word gets out. A favorable reputation will precede you wherever you go. You want your reputation to be an asset. Conversely, a bad reputation can be your worst negotiating debit.

In my mind, integrity is the lifeblood of your reputation. If you have integrity, your word will be your bond. You can't develop a reputation for going back on your word, even if it means getting a lesser deal. If people know that you will go back on your word, there is no chance of creating a favorable atmosphere. If you change your ethics as often as your socks, you'll be pegged as unreliable and dishonest. A good reputation is central to creating that right atmosphere.

As an attorney, I believe in the sanctity of contracts. If you make a commitment, fulfill it. That's what I tell my clients. When they sign a contract, I expect them to honor the agreement they've signed. Let me tell you about what happened with Julius Erving.

I lost Julius as a client early in his career when he demanded a renegotiation with the Virginia Squires of the American Basketball Association. I had negotiated a $125,000-a-year contract for him, and during his first season because he was playing well, he decided he wanted a new contract which would pay him a lot more. I didn't think it was right. I said to him, "If you had a terrible year, would you go in and return fifteen thousand dollars?"

"What do you think I am, crazy?" said Julius.

"Then why would you expect them to pay you more now? They didn't pay you to play badly. They paid you to play well."

The logic didn't work and Julius decided to find another representative to do the job for him. I was sorry to see him go, but not if it meant compromising my beliefs and, consequently, my reputation. I firmly believe that people who honor their contracts turn out better than those who don't. I don't think Julius was ever paid what his talent deserved, and I think that was due to his constant, career-long demands that his contracts be renegotiated after the fact. Incidentally, despite our disagreement, Julius and I are still good friends all these years later, which goes to show not only do you not have to be disagreeable to disagree, if you do disagree, your relations need not be disagreeable!

It Helps To Be Trusted

If people trust you and you are careful not to violate that trust, there isn't anything that can't be accomplished. Wars start when people and countries don't trust each other. It is possible to reach an agreement even if the parties don't trust each other. But if they do, it will be a lot easier to come to a fairer, more equitable agreement.

A perfect example of trust involves two men from different worlds who found common ground: Ted Turner and Fidel Castro.

I can assure you that Turner is one of a kind: bold, outspoken, flamboyant, quick-tempered, engaging, unpredictable, and surprisingly open-minded. He is one passionate Southern conservative who has pursued his own peace initiative with the Soviet Union and Cuba.

In the business world, Ted Turner is a Renaissance man who broke new ground with his Cable News Network and Atlanta-based superstation, Turner Broadcasting Service. His attempted takeover of CBS kept that network in turmoil for months and sent its stock skyrocketing. Although he did not invent junk bonds, he made the phrase a familiar one long before it caught everyone's attention on Wall Street.

In sports, Turner has captured the headlines by winning the America's Cup as skipper of the yacht *Courageous*. His antics in that realm and others soon led to the colorful and often appropriate nickname, "Captain Outrageous." Turner owns Atlanta's basketball team, the Hawks, as well as the city's baseball team, the Braves. He even spent one game in the dugout as the Braves' acting manager, an action that incurred the wrath of the commissioner of baseball. But then, it's not unusual for his actions to upset someone—or everyone.

Turner was willing to lose $10 million on his sponsorship of the Olympics-style Goodwill Games in Moscow in July, 1986, where American and Russian athletes competed on a world stage for the first time in eight years. That effort met with opposition from his own government and ridicule from much of the world press. Typically, neither response deterred Ted Turner.

In short, Turner is a dynamic character, a man of wealth and influence who does not follow conventional paths. Where other businessmen may prefer to develop a quieter image, aligning themselves with culture and the arts, Turner has immersed himself in the popular arena where he willfully prides himself, sometimes quite literally, on being a boat-rocker. When he bought the MGM film library and proceeded to "colorize" black-and-white classics like *Casablanca* and *The Maltese Falcon* for play on TBS, film purists ranging from directors John Huston to Woody Allen howled in protest. Turner's response to the critics? Turn off the color and watch 'em in black and white.

Having observed him in action over the course of several negotiations, I have come to know Turner as an outgoing and genuinely amiable man. He is a populist who likes to see and be seen. This sets him apart from many of his peers. You don't see New York Yankees' owner George Steinbrenner in shirtsleeves driving his own Toyota around town. People don't wave to CBS founder William Paley in the streets and shout, "Hi, Bill!" and ask for autographs.

Turner can be impulsive and explains away his often outrageous statements by saying, "Sometimes when I talk my brain is not in gear." However, he is secure among the powerful and comfortable with the famous. He consistently tries to be gracious to strangers.

Turner has the endless capacity to surprise you. He can argue with someone over a deal all day, then invite them to share his seats at the ballpark at night and divulge his confidences on unrelated business matters. Where some owners' seats are tucked away in the luxury boxes, Turner prefers to sit right out where his players and fans can see him— and he can see them—in the field boxes that jut onto Atlanta Fulton County Stadium, almost like a jetty.

Ted is always in touch. There is no pretense in him. If he is feeling irritated or grumpy, he will tell you about it. This is a straightforward fellow, and, having come to that conclusion, I find it advisable to approach him in the same way: head-on. Turner is exciting but not foolhardy. He would spend money to get what he wants, but you have to convince him that the money is justified.

Turner reinforced some of my long-held beliefs about negotiating, such as sending the right man for the right job and gaining trust and justifying that portal of trustworthiness.

Could anyone imagine a less likely pair than Ted Turner and Fidel Castro? Yet it developed.

It seems that the Cuban premier believes that Cable News Network gives his country more fair coverage than any other American news network. On that basis, and given their common interests in sports— Turner, the yachtsman and team owner; Fidel, a onetime baseball pitcher who fancied a big-league career—Castro invited Turner to visit Havana as his guest.

56

Between the more formal aspects of the visit, the two men broke away for a day of hunting and fishing. I sat in Turner's office, spellbound by his videotape of the trip and his personal narration. I listened as he told me about his private time with the leader of a Communist nation ninety miles from our shores, a man whose political system Turner himself considered anathema to our own.

There they were, the Cuban dictator and the maverick capitalist, hunting birds, alone on a small boat in a Caribbean lake, laughing, joking, *each holding a loaded rifle*.

It is widely known that the Central Intelligence Agency hatched many a plot to assassinate Castro over the past thirty years, and Castro is not careless about his security. This is a man whose staff plucked their own chickens rather than risk getting poisoned when he visited the United Nations in the early '60s. It occurred to me to allow an American that kind of lethal access was indeed a remarkable show of faith.

What is interesting here is not whether Turner could have acted uncharacteristically, but that Castro was indifferent to the possibility because of his basic trust in Ted Turner. Do you know what all this tells me? That quite possibly, Ted Turner could better represent the United States in negotiations with Cuba than any politician we could name today.

In their brief time together, Castro had come to trust the wealthy capitalist magnate. He knew that Turner could be tough and opinionated, but that he was an honorable man. This just goes to show that the right reputation combined with the right atmosphere can reverse even the most inauspicious negotiating conditions.

Some Things Are Worth More than Money—Celtic Pride

When you're creating a balance sheet on which to judge the issues, you should give strong consideration to reputation, motivation, production, success, camaraderie, style, trust, compassion, honor, and respect—all the components which offer you dignity. You may find that some things are worth more than money.

"Celtic Pride," which has fueled the remarkable Boston Celtics organization for many decades, is built on this principle. By creating an environment which both respects the individual and demands personal sacrifice toward a greater group goal, the Celtics created one of America's most successful organizations.

They have maintained this success for over thirty years by rewarding the team and the men. When the Celtics have needed an experienced point guard or a solid back-up center, they have made a priority of obtaining them, thereby strengthening each player in his quest for a championship.

When a player has contributed significantly to the historic success of the franchise, sometimes they may permit him to play at top salary for a year longer than normal, and after his retirement ceremoniously raise his jersey number in honor, to hang in recognition over the parquet floor.

There are plenty of players who would gladly have taken a reduction in pay just to have been able to play for and with the World Champion Boston Celtics. The Celtics have consistently been able to control their payroll by using dignity and pride as currency rather than cash.

They did this most significantly with John Havlicek. In 1969, after seven years in the NBA and six league championships with the Celtics, "Hondo's" contract came up for renewal. He was a four-time all-star who had led the Celtics that season in scoring, assists, and minutes played. With this endless hustle, tireless work, and wholesome character, Havlicek had established himself with the Boston fans and management as a man very much in the celebrated and revered "Celtic tradition." The Celtics were family and he had become the favorite son.

The American Basketball Association, two seasons old and looking to make inroads into the more established league's territory, saw Havlicek for what he was: the very best the NBA had to offer. His brand of great basketball and personal integrity could help put the ABA on the map. They offered him $1.2 million cash to jump leagues and play three seasons in the ABA. The Celtics were paying Havlicek $85,000 a year.

This was an offer that could not be ignored. During the negotiating, which began with the ABA offering $50,000 a year for 40 years (a "$2 million contract," in concept only, when you factor in inflation and lost interest), ABA commissioner Jim Gardner would call each morning at eight o'clock and increase their total package by $150,000. An hour later, Red Auerbach, then the Celtics' general manager and keeper of the flame, would call and say, "Bob, do you think another two hundred and fifty dollars would help the situation?" Red was having a hard time getting a grasp on the seriousness of the ABA's competition.

The ABA needed Havlicek. As a result, they agreed to clauses in his proposed contract that had not yet been commonly won for players in the NBA: if the team or league folded, or John was disabled, he would still receive the $1.2 million in full; a certain amount would be placed in escrow; a surety performance bond would guarantee payment; the ABA owners, with a combined net worth in the hundreds of millions of dollars, would sign as individual guarantors. Hondo could also pick the team he would play for, and he could not be traded without his consent.

The Celtics responded to what at the time was the greatest bid ever offered an athlete by submitting one for $750,000 less: $150,000 a year for three years. It was the largest Celtics proposal in history, more than Bill Russell or Bob Cousy had made at the height of their careers. In that sense it was flattering, but it was nowhere near the ABA's package.

As negotiations progressed, the ABA was pressing us for an answer, but I insisted that Havlicek allow the Celtics to make the last offer. We were to meet in Auerbach's office and I asked John to bring his wife, Beth. I knew he would want her there and her presence would remind Red that this was a family decision. It might also restrain his legendary temper.

There was the usual reading-of-the-will uneasiness as we settled into the chairs in front of Red's desk. It was impossible to sit in that room and not feel an almost tangible sense of Celtic tradition and Celtic pride. Photographs of Celtics' glories covered one wall and the room was a jumble of trophies and plaques, tokens of eleven NBA championships in thirteen years.

After recapping our positions, I said, "Red, I'm through negotiating with the ABA. I know what we have there, and a decision will be made here, this afternoon. The ABA has offered John over a million dollars. I'm not suggesting the Celtics pay that. I just want you to have all the facts."

Auerbach nodded. He was not happy, feeling I had used the ABA offer as leverage to break his salary curve. But he was polite. We talked for over an hour and in response to the ABA's lavish figures and the unsettling possibility that the team would lose the prototypical Celtic, Red raised his offer to $600,000 for three years.

Then he stood up and said calmly, "Okay, this is as far as I can go. If I go any further, it will throw off my salary structure completely. Take a few minutes to think it over." I understood his position. He left the room to let us make our decision.

I turned to Havlicek. "This is your decision," I said. "It's your life. All I know is that right now there isn't anyone who can say a harsh word about John Havlicek. But just understand this. If you should jump, there is a small segment of the population that will think unkindly of you."

John and Beth talked softly together for about ten minutes. Then John put a hand on my shoulder. "Look, Bob," he said. "I've worked all my life. I've always tried to do what was right. I never, believe me, thought I would earn more than twenty-five thousand dollars a year in anything I did. I just can't believe these sums of money we're talking about here.

"But to tell you the truth, I love Boston. I love Red Auerbach and everything the Celtics stand for. I value my reputation. I value what I think is right. So my answer is this. Even if they offered me two and a half million, I would stay with the Boston Celtics."

Red Auerbach and the Celtics organization had created the opportunity for John Havlicek to live what at one time would have seemed to him a fantasy life. They had encouraged him and developed his talents, given him respect and the foundation on which to gain even more; they had paid him well and treated him as he wanted to be treated. By dealing with dignity, the Celtics upheld their tradition. When the time came to make a choice, Havlicek decided he would rather have the dignity of being a Celtic than have an extra half-million dollars.

I didn't argue with that decision for a moment.

CHAPTER THREE

Preparation

"Luck is when preparation meets opportunity."

—a wise NFL coach's advice

"The way to do things is to begin."

—HORACE GREELEY

"Great battles are won before they are actually fought."

—JOHN LUBBOCK

YOU CAN be a champion negotiator if you prepare properly. Most people just walk into a negotiation and fire away. "I need a raise," or "What will you take for this house?" It is critical that you do your homework. The trick is to acquire all the information concerning the issues involved, even ones you may not deem as important at a glance. How well you prepare depends on the volume and quality of the information you gather.

63

Why? Because in negotiating, *information translates to power*. The more facts and knowledge you have, the more viable your position.

You can't always outsmart someone, but you *can* outprepare them. Think of getting information as your chance to play detective or investigative reporter; you're Philip Marlowe or Bob Woodward digging up the information you need for a client or a story. The work can be tedious, exhilarating, and repetitive, but the tougher the negotiation, the more dogged you'll have to be.

So, *don't be lazy*. Ask the next question. Research a little longer. Make that extra call. Review your approach one more time.

Throughout the years, I have been fortunate to represent some of the greatest athletes in the world. I've represented players who have won practically every sports award ever given: the Heisman Trophy, the Cy Young Award, the Maxwell Award, the John Wooden Award, the Joe Lapchick Award, Most Valuable Player awards, inductions to the various Halls of Fame.

In analyzing what makes a champion, I have come to the conclusion that what these athletes have in common is extraordinary commitment, singlemindedness of purpose, mental toughness, unusual self-discipline, and above all, they *prepare* far beyond anybody else.

We all know ballet dancers work vigorously on a daily basis to hone their skills. Pro golfers go to the driving range. Tennis stars work on their serves for hours a day. But I'm not talking about mere practice. I'm talking about a greater effort, a step further—real *preparation*.

I have seen Formula One race car drivers who go around the track before race day so they will know later, when they are at full throttle, where to take the inside lines that win races and where to double clutch to avoid the curves that can kill them. Certain actors go to extraordinary lengths in preparation for a role. Tom Cruise spent months in an Air Force fighter cockpit learning to be a pilot for the movie *Top Gun*. Meryl Streep learned to speak Polish to perfect her accent for the title role in *Sophie's Choice*.

I have watched Carl Yastrzemski of the Boston Red Sox spend hours taking countless fungo balls off the Green Monster, the nearly impossible-to-play, thirty-seven-foot-high left field green wall at Fenway Park that has confounded nearly every player who has ever played at the venerated old stadium. Early in his career, Yastrzemski said, "The wall can make you feel like you've never played baseball before, but I'm going to know that wall better than anyone in baseball."

Yaz said that Ted Williams, his predecessor as the Red Sox left fielder, had never told him much about the wall, and even if he had, it wouldn't have made much difference. He knew he had to do his own preparation. He began by studying the construction of the wall.

"The first twenty-five feet is concrete," he says. "Then you come up to the thin part which has two-by-four steel girders behind it with rivets that hold the tin in. I have to make a decision as soon as the ball hits in the rivet area whether I'm going to move to my right or my left, but I have to take into account if the batter who hits it is left-handed or right-handed so I can figure out the spin factor once it hits the wall, or the rivets, or the two-by-fours. Each surface makes the ball carom in a different direction. If the ball hits the concrete, it will come flying back at me hard, but if it hits the tin area, it will just drop straight down."

Yaz was determined to "own" that wall, so he also studied all its scratches and bumps so he wouldn't be surprised during a game by any odd angles created by such imperfections. It was no accident that Carl was named to the American League All-Star team eighteen times, won six Gold Glove Awards and was inducted into the Baseball Hall of Fame. He is a master of preparation.

Larry Bird of the Boston Celtics also takes preparation very seriously. Once, in the off-season, we went to work out in a local gym. We ran a series of wind sprints and afterward, while I was still huffing and puffing, he said, "I really got a good feel for the court."

"What do you mean?" I asked.

"When I run," he said, "I count my steps, so that when I get to midcourt, I know exactly how many steps it takes to get to my twenty-one-foot shot, to my eighteen-foot shot, and to my fifteen-footer. I take three steps and I know exactly where I am. I don't have to look. I'll also know how many steps to a certain place where I can make a certain pass. My back can be facing the basket, but I still know exactly where I am."

Here I'd just been running up and down the court. I'd thought Larry was doing the same, but he was far ahead of me. It wasn't until that day that I realized that for all of his seemingly spontaneous wizardry on the court, Larry Bird's "blind" passes aren't blind at all.

I have also gone to Boston Garden several hours before a game and watched Larry shoot for two hours and then kneel down on the parquet floor to inspect the bolts that connect the wooden squares of the basketball floor. When I asked him later what he had been doing, he explained to me that he inspects the floor just that way before every game to find out which bolts might be loose. Such bolts could affect the way the ball bounces when he dribbles on the fast break. By this time before the game, he had also already dribbled the ball over the whole court to determine the dead spots that he might use to his advantage during the game and the spots he should avoid altogether. He confided in me that when he sees the opposing player dribbling the ball in the area of one of those dead spots, he always goes for the steal because he knows the other player, not expecting the odd bounce, can lose control of the ball more easily. *This* is what I call preparation.

Bird has a million shots and he knows every arc and every type of spin on other people's shots as well as his own. He watches the ball spin as it's in the air and he knows, before it hits the backboard or rim, which way it will carom. Every teenage pick-up game, his college experience, and his entire pro career are all preparation for that one critical moment when the game is in the balance and he must come down with the ball. And this rebound is more preparation for the next one.

Larry's game begins well before the opening tip-off. Sometimes, Larry will scare me to death when we'll walk on the court and all of a sudden, he will throw himself down—this incredibly valuable six-foot-ten man hitting the hard, shiny floor—just to get used to falling on that particular court. I'm sure you've seen boxers get into the ring and start hitting themselves in the face, or two football players pushing each other on the sidelines to get used to the feeling. This is Larry's version.

66

So you can see, the champions go the extra mile in preparation and try to get as much information as they can. Remember, *information is power*. A negotiation doesn't begin when the opposing sides finally sit down face-to-face. A truly well-conceived negotiation actually starts when the strategies are developed, the positions planned and, even further back, when the goals are first decided upon. Before all negotiations, major or minor, I go over in my mind what I want, what my opponent's needs are, what my market value is, and what else I know that might possibly make what I want come more easily.

In order to enhance my position, I need a full inventory of information concerning all the issues involved, from money to working conditions to perquisites, chances for advancement, potential roadblocks or speed traps. I need to know the quickest route to my goal and the slowest; who has traveled this road before me and the ease or difficulty of their ride, and how I can safely and effectively enter the fast lane. I want to know everything I can about myself, my client, and the parties involved on the other side.

Assessing Fair Market Value

In preparing for a negotiation, I try to research the fair market value for the goods or services at hand, so that my proposal is a realistic one. The "fair market value" is whatever is normally paid for someone's services or for a product. Probably the most important piece of information you can ascertain will be the fair market value. The term is significant because it helps you establish what a fair and reasonable price is to pay, or to be paid, for goods and services.

The best way to determine fair market value is to ask people in the industry, whether it's a short-term, high-stakes field like professional sports or entertainment, or a less volatile field with longevity like most office jobs. Try to speak to experts in the particular field, such as real estate agents when you are buying a house, or employment consultants when you are looking for a job. There are norms and people familiar with the industry know them. Remember, *it doesn't hurt to ask*.

If you work in a large organization, it is wise to get out in the field and look around. For a long time, baseball clubs would go out of their way to make sure their players didn't find out what other players were making. Teammates knew each other's batting averages, stolen bases, and RBIs, but they didn't know each other's salaries. They did not have the information or ammunition to say to a general manager, "Look, you're paying Sparky twenty-seven thousand dollars. I outhit him by thirty points, knocked in twenty more runs and stole five more bases, and you're only paying me nineteen thousand five hundred dollars. I think I deserve a raise."

Most offices are still the same way; it is impolite to ask, "What are you making?" When in fact, it's a very important question to have answered before you negotiate with your boss for a raise. If you and a co-worker are performing approximately the same tasks and he is being paid twice your salary, you ought to be aware of the situation so that you can readjust your financial thinking. The fact that the company values that work at $60,000 and you are getting only $30,000 is reason to ask for an increase. You would never know to pursue that extra money if you did not know what the company was paying and you won't find out without asking. This is a clear case of information equaling power. Employees might demand higher, commensurate wages if they are aware of salary discrepancies.

The main reason most people won't say what they're making is pride; nobody wants to risk being low man on the totem pole. Therefore, you have to find a way of asking that will not offend your co-workers. And you should be prepared to be as honest with them as you are asking them to be with you. Tell them your figure or offer some kind of information equally valuable to them. Offer to keep their salary confidential, but make it clear that the information you are gathering will benefit everybody. If you are making more than most people on your level, they will have the opportunity to readjust their sights. If they are outearning you, you will have grounds to ask for more. It is only the employer trying to keep costs down who may be faced with a problem.

I consistently get calls from other representatives, and even from athletes I do not represent, asking if this figure or that stipulation they have been offered is in line with what is standard in the industry. It is information I am happy to share; if they can top my figures or add other benefits to a contract which I have not successfully incorporated into mine, I have a higher floor from which to negotiate in the future. The more other people are making in my field—the more the field is valuing its own work—the more my clients stand to make.

Luckily, from a variety of experiences, I've been able to accumulate a lot of information. For instance, I have the contracts of every player in major league baseball, football, and basketball as well as most hockey salaries. I know their salaries, bonuses, and incentive clauses. I remember with relish the shocked looks on the faces of general managers when I presented them with their team's entire salary lists as I argued for my client's salary request. They often ask if they can keep my master list for the team. They've never had all that information in one place before.

Getting the Key Information

Fortunately, getting the information necessary for you to determine the fair market value isn't always difficult to get. So much is available from public sources, or by simply asking people intelligent questions. Remember, *it doesn't hurt to ask.*

Of course, everyday situations like purchasing groceries or buying shoes don't require a Sherlock Holmes-style inquiry. But nevertheless, it doesn't hurt to check the newspapers for discount coupons or special sales for your best prices and values.

But a more intricate maneuver, such as a corporate takeover, a deal with a new network executive, or buying a car or boat will likely require you to make a special effort to contact "sources," both public and private. Quite simply, you will open the door to failure if you don't know as much as possible when you negotiate. An investment banker is ineffectual without full knowledge of the state of the company he is advising, the state of the economy, and the status of the stock and bond markets and interest rates before issuing millions of dollars in corporate equities.

A car buyer is at a complete disadvantage if he or she doesn't shop at various dealerships and read *Consumer Reports* and Jack Gillis's annual *The Car Book* to become acquainted with the range of options in purchasing a car. For a used car, *The Blue Book* is the bible of prices. Every car dealer values a car differently. The base price may be set by the manufacturer, but the way options are valued can make a difference. Some dealers may have more options available from their manufacturer and can be more price-flexible. One dealer may be willing to throw in (often free) electric windows or a better radio than the car generally comes with. If you're seeking an advantage, you might want to make a dealership contact through a friend who has just bought a car there. Or, even better, you might have a friend who has bought several cars there for his business. If your friend is a consistent buyer, he may get a price break. If you find out his discounted price, then perhaps you can get that lower price, too. Think of it as discount by association.

Your search for knowledge might also include reading newspaper accounts about a car company's sales inventory. The bigger the inventory, the more likely a dealer is to compromise. You could go back to the same dealer several times and find that little or nothing has been sold in two or three weeks. Many times, dealers in more rural areas have lower overhead expenses and can offer lower prices than their metropolitan counterparts. Assiduous research can save you money. Additional knowledge can make your negotiations go much more smoothly.

Certainly, a prospective home buyer interested in a particular house will be met with unpleasant surprises if he or she isn't familiar with recent sales on the block, how long the house has been on the market, the true condition of the house, the quality of neighborhood schools, any upcoming real estate tax reassessments, liens, or easements on the property, state taxes, zoning laws, and any commercial buildings to be built in the area.

Comparably, anyone seeking a raise will not likely succeed if he or she doesn't have a complete record of his or her work and solid information on what people in similar positions are currently earning, including bonuses and/or profit sharing, vacation time, medical benefits, and retirement plans for a realistic base of comparison.

Know Your Client

Once I have confidence that I have arrived at the fair market value for the services of my client through my research, I want to *research all of the personalities involved*.

If you are representing someone other than yourself, you want to know what his values are. What are his goals? What is important to him in life? Become a student of his ego, character, intentions, temperament, idiosyncrasies, and attitudes. This form of preparation requires deeper digging, but it remains a crucial point of advance work. It is a mistake to assume that your client's goals and values are identical to what your own would be, given his situation. You can't even assume his aims are comparable to his colleagues or peers.

For example, most of the television or radio performers I represent are thrilled for any additional public exposure that may happen to come their way. But my client Gene Shalit, the popular and witty movie critic on NBC's "The Today Show," feels very differently. Gene is a very private and modest man. Rather than court the camera's glare, he avoids all intrusions into his personal affairs, preferring to appear before the public only in his line of work.

Consequently, I keep Gene's penchant for privacy ever in mind. So I have negotiated contracts for him with NBC that limit the days he is on the air. In addition, in response to the many endorsement requests for Gene, I keep his commitment to a minimum. I end up doing the reverse of what I would normally do for an entertainment client because I am aware of this particular client's preferences. My main aim is to keep him satisfied.

It helps to know if your client has a high profile temperament, the kind of person who needs the best in clothes and cars, and enjoys a little fanfare, or if he is tight with a dollar or a free spender. I make it a point to learn all I can about him as a human being: his ego, his complexes, and his superstitions. You might ask yourself, how can knowing someone's personality traits help me prepare for a negotiation? Would it really matter what my client's beliefs, behavior, and superstitions are? The answer is, everything matters.

Insights into a client's character can prepare you for his response to the negotiations. Will he make a judgment on the basis of something other than the facts? Does he think he is smarter than everybody else at the table? His ego will tell you whether or not he should even be present for the negotiations, whether he will be an asset or should be kept at arm's length. Is he going to be supportive of your efforts? Even if he means well, will he in any way be a negative influence?

When I was practicing criminal law, I had clients whose appearances were so unfavorable, I knew I couldn't risk my case by putting them on the stand. They might have been completely innocent, but they *appeared to be guilty*. They had a poor way of speaking. Their nervousness made them seem shifty.

Rather than ignore their shortcomings, pretending they weren't there, I paid careful attention to them. Since I was representing these people's interests, I was better off acknowledging their strengths and weaknesses in formulating a strategy. There are times when maintaining a positive attitude for optimism's sake is simply irresponsible. Better to catalog shortcomings than to turn a blind eye to them, only to be tripped up by them later.

By knowing everything you can about your client, you can often avoid potentially crippling mistakes. Can he take the pressure? If I am handling a negotiation for him, can I bring him into the room or would I be better off keeping him out? A lot of people can compete in front of thousands of fans and knock the tar out of someone, but they'll freeze in a courtroom, in a hospital, or across a conference table. Once, in the middle of contract talks, a rugged ice hockey player, the Detroit Red Wings' Mickey Redmond, who had scored fifty-two goals in a season, listened to the arguments back and forth and ended up fainting in my arms.

The Rasputin Factor

Knowing who influences or surrounds your client is extremely important. Is your client going to be listening to someone else? One of the most taxing experiences I've ever had was with a basketball player who just didn't have enough confidence in his own counsel and leaned too much on the advice of his strong-willed wife. It turned what should have been a pleasant negotiation into a difficult experience.

The player, now a star, was pure magic on the court. He was in the enviable position of being a free agent, available to talk to any team. I had been talking with several teams interested in negotiating for his services for an extended period of time.

After negotiating with the various teams, we settled on one whose general manager offered to pay my client $3 million over four years, with a $500,000 signing bonus. My client seemed very happy with the final proposal. Together we made plans to fly to the team's city and sign the contract. However, the morning after we had reached an agreement, my client called to tell me that he couldn't make the trip with me because his wife was not happy with the terms.

His wife got on the phone and announced, "We're not signing the contract. I don't mind the signing bonus and the last year at one million dollars is fine. But I only want a three-year contract with five hundred thousand dollars more, and another thing, I want the team to pay our rent and provide me with a new winter wardrobe because it's cold there."

This stance was difficult at best. The general manager was quite volatile and I knew he wouldn't respond warmly to these new demands. He was ready to pay my client more than any player in his team's history, but I doubted he would go so far as to accede to this woman's demand for a winter wardrobe. I managed to persuade my client and his wife to accompany me to the team's offices, where, I assured them, I would try to get more accommodations in the contract.

I sat down with the general manager, who thought we were just going to calmly sign the contract. Instead, I had to present some new terms to him. He had no idea how the wife had changed the course of the negotiation. But he found out quickly enough. We did our best to ignore her persistent outbursts while trying to appease her with some creative changes in the contract's wording. After a while, I sensed that the manager had gone as far as he was willing to go. Even though the player's wife was still not satisfied, I had to turn to my client and say, "This is the best deal you are going to get, and I'm afraid your wife is going to ruin it all."

Luckily, my client had enough trust in me to break the logjam and agree to the contract, much to my relief.

In this case, I hadn't been adequately prepared. I hadn't known enough about the player's wife to anticipate her demands, nor did I realize the kind of influence she wielded over him. Had I known, it would have spared me some difficult and unpleasant surprises. Sometimes, such developments are unavoidable. You have to learn on the run and adapt when events change around you, much the way a good jazz pianist does instinctively when the guitarist starts improvising. But anytime you can reduce unexpected surprises by asking the right questions ahead of time, you are that much ahead of the game.

So I also need to know whether a client is likely to be influenced, or misled, by perhaps a third party working in the shadows. If I am handling my client's money, I insist on acquainting myself with those around him, particularly any potential source of bad information or advice. And remember, at issue is not whether these advisors would influence you. The question remains, would they influence your client? Historically, ill advice has come in a variety of unlikely sectors. It was

Rasputin, the wild-eyed religious zealot, whose advice to the Tsar and Tsarina helped bring the Russian monarchy down.

What are your client's outside commitments, potential distractions, his habits? Is he involved with drugs? Does he have a history of legal problems? Arrests? Paternity suits? I can assure you nothing will dampen a negotiation as quickly as a police rap sheet on your client presented at the very moment you are singing his praises. If I've spent months developing a liquor endorsement for an entertainer whom I represent, later is not the time I want to discover that he has a drinking problem.

I need to know if the client is going to be the kind who:

- travels to Cleveland on a road trip, buys $4,000 worth of clothes one afternoon, then leaves the city having left all his new clothes in the closet of the room he never checked out of, resulting in a $3,000 hotel bill a month later.
- rents two cars in the same day and abandons them on two different streets, leaving you talking to Hertz on one line and Avis on the other, both wanting to know where their cars are.
- buys a new set of golf clubs at a country club, plays one round of golf and then gives the clubs to his caddie as a tip.
- calls my office in Boston from his hotel room in Hawaii to ask me to call the general manager of the hotel to complain that he doesn't have enough hot water in his room.
- calls, in the throes of a drug problem, from San Diego, to say he has been kidnapped and chained to a bed, has wriggled free just enough to reach the telephone and tell you that his captors are going to kill him if he does not have $10,000 there in thirty minutes.
- may be having some drug problems because every time he steps to the foul line during a game, he takes several steps in *front* of the line as he puts up his shot.
- wouldn't fly in for his contract signing unless the team flew in his dog as well.
- calls me in Boston at 2 A.M. from a Los Angeles nightclub where

it's only 11 P.M. asking you to wire him $5,000 so he can invest in a "sure thing" that is personally guaranteed by his latest new-found "friend."

These vignettes are brought to you by one who has experienced each and every one of them. What do these examples of erratic behavior mean to me as a negotiator? They put me on notice to structure the contract *to protect my client against himself.* Perhaps I'll try to put in more deferred monies he can't immediately touch, or include annuities that will be beyond his immediate reach, and to think of as many safeguards as I can that will be in his best interest.

It is essential to know if he has relatives who are going to make a run at him if he comes into money. Is he the type to give out loans? Does he have a brother-in-law whose business is in trouble? Do I have to protect this person from himself? I want to know all this and more: is he frivolous? Does he go from woman to woman, as an old ballad says, the way "a silver dollar goes from hand to hand"? Are you going to be receiving bills for diamonds and other expensive trinkets?

The more information you have, the better able you are to provide for the client's future. How do you obtain this information? You ask. Ask the client. Ask his family and friends. Don't be afraid to ask him and those who know him what his habits are.

There is another question I want answered: Does my client have character? If I negotiate a four-year contract, is he going to sleepwalk through the first three years and then play like a whiz the final year, as I have seen athletes do? Or is he the kind of player who will give his all—or just his almost? Is he going to come back and ask that the contract be renegotiated, in effect, breaking his word?

If I have prepared a contract that includes incentives, is he going to be thinking only of reaching them, or will he aspire to triumphs beyond? Is he going to be so concerned with how many touchdown passes he has to catch to earn those incentives, that he becomes less of a ballplayer? Many times I will avoid such incentives in my client's interest, if I don't think he will respond to them properly.

76

Know Yourself

Do you have an interest that would hurt your client? Is there a conflict of interest? Is there some reason not under your control that renders you ineffective to do the best job for your client? Is there someone else in your office who could handle it better?

If you are negotiating for yourself, examine your own ego and your emotions. Will you fly off the handle or tend to insult the other party? If so, and if you feel you will be unable to control your actions, then perhaps, at those times, you should let someone else negotiate for you.

Is there someone in your family, a friend, who could be less impassioned? If you do choose a friend or family member, exercise caution and assess their ability to remain unemotional on your behalf. Hopefully, after you have finished this book, you will be able to handle any negotiation with more confidence. But even experienced negotiators have encountered times when they had to step aside. For instance, I can remember when Larry King called me to represent him even though his best friend was Herb Cohen, a highly successful professional negotiator. Larry explained to me that Herb Cohen had told him that as much as he would have liked to work with Larry that he probably would not be the best person to represent him in his contract negotiations. Herb felt that because of their exceptionally close friendship he cared too much— almost like a surgeon who would be reluctant to operate on his own child.

Know Your Opponent

Once I have examined my side, it is time to research the other side just as carefully. Think of yourself as a scout, following a rival baseball team for a few days before they come to play in your ballpark. You'll want to know how the other team's hitters and pitchers perform; whether their game is fundamentally sound; how their pitchers hold on runners and how the hitters lay down sacrifice bunts.

Why are you doing this? To understand your opponent, so that when you face him, you'll be prepared. You'll know how he generally behaves in most situations. You may not have a chance to get to know him as an insider, but you can get to know him well enough to develop the most winning strategy.

Research his general background. What is his experience, intelligence, upbringing, and interests? If it's a business entity or a corporate executive you are dealing with, check the *Forbes* 400, the *Fortune* 500, *Who's Who In America*, *Dun & Bradstreet*, or the Better Business Bureau to gain more information. *Who's Who*, for instance, will list a person's age, education, family members, employment history, club and association memberships. You can go through newspapers and magazines at your local library for more extensive background reports.

From some of these sources, you can probably find some people your adversary has dealt with in the past—bankers, manufacturers, retailers, and attorneys. People are more approachable than you think; call some of them. Ask them what your prospective negotiating partner is like. Is he tough? Fair? A lunatic? Some of these people will no doubt be skittish about talking, especially if the person you are inquiring about is a close friend or associate. But remember, *it doesn't hurt to ask*.

In some cases, your research might also yield a bonus: someone who doesn't like the person. Reporters love finding this kind of source—the archetypal disgruntled employee—for although they may bear a distinct prejudice, the information you can glean may be quite rich.

Don't overlook the opportunity to make inquiries of people close to your opponent. If you get a chance, chat with the secretary. I've learned plenty from secretaries, little tidbits I've used in a variety of ways. One team owner's secretary once told me about a huge, celebrity-filled party at her boss's house the previous weekend. Before the negotiation began, I said to the owner, "Was the party that big? Did so-and-so really do that!" This lighter moment created a happy starting point for our talks. The owner was obviously flattered that I had heard about his extravaganza and was only too pleased to regale me with anecdotes about it.

I like to know my partner's reputation. Is he known as being fair? Some negotiators relish the battle, the tangle of wits, the crossing of swords. They will try to take the heart out of you. Be prepared. Is he the kind who rants and raves? Whose voice can frighten fowl on the Charles River? When I negotiate with Red Auerbach, I know he will call me every name in the book and a few that are still pending. You just sit back and wait him out. Common sense tells you that the more you know about such tendencies, the more prepared you will be to deal with them.

What are his personal characteristics? Any biases, quirky habits, idiosyncrasies, prejudices, bad temper, or phobias? Is he flamboyant? If so, he may have the tendency to spend his organization's money more freely.

There is one general manager in one of the pro sports leagues who is most receptive to working out the terms of an agreement when he is, shall we say, not quite sober. So if you have a contract to negotiate, you know there is no point in pressing the issue until after dinner and a few drinks. Fortunately, this GM always remembers the next morning what commitment he made the previous night.

In my line of business, I have come to understand the personality profiles of many of the people I deal with. Successful businessmen in high-profit, low-visibility industries decide to invest their finances, indulge their fantasies and make a name for themselves by purchasing professional sports franchises. Where only months before, they may have put together multimillion-dollar, even multibillion-dollar deals and nobody heard about them, their every move suddenly makes the papers day after day. They could pay a press agent a million dollars a year and not approach the immense popularity they achieve for a simple gesture like acquiring a hot-hitting third baseman.

Gene Klein, who sold his NFL San Diego Chargers after becoming disenchanted with the league's business practices and practitioners, said, "Many people buy a sports franchise simply as an ego sop. You take a man who has made one hundred million dollars in real estate or the shipbuilding business, nobody knows who he is. He's just another person who's made one hundred million dollars. You buy a sports team, and boom—you're a national figure."

I have found the typical owner to be a man who has made his fortune in unrelated fields, and is searching for something that would yield recognition, prestige, and some fun.

And for some it actually works that way. Sonny Werblin, who built the New York Jets and helped establish the American Football League, was one of the most powerful businessmen in the country for two decades before he bought into pro football. He ran the Music Corporation of America, whose show business clientele included Frank Sinatra, Cary Grant, and Elizabeth Taylor. But until Sonny Werblin brought Joe Willie Namath to Broadway and the New York Jets, he was little known outside his own business circles. Then Sonny himself became a star.

Phil Wrigley, the late owner of the Chicago Cubs, whose product exercised the jaws of Americans for three generations, marveled at the process. "I make a multimillion-dollar deal in business," he once said, "and I get two paragraphs in *The Wall Street Journal* the next day. I fire Leo Durocher, and it's front page news all over the country."

Wrigley, a private, almost reclusive person, became a sports celebrity in spite of himself. Small wonder that those who seem to seek the spotlight always find it. Once, the owner was someone who stayed in the background and let the "experts" run his business. They came around a few times a year to accept a plaque from the chamber of commerce or check to see if anyone had stolen the ballpark. But now there is a new breed of owners who love to get involved with their players and be recognized in public.

It has become evident to me that if someone has control of or in any way influences the leisure time of people, then they become instant celebrities themselves. The position creates the power. I've always felt that if a truly wealthy man wanted a shortcut to national celebrity, all he would really have to do is own a major league baseball franchise in Washington, D.C., and invite the political hierarchy of the country to sit in his private box and watch the team. A franchise in the nation's capital offers the highest possible visibility at a price that, on balance, might be considered a true bargain.

One of the most perceptive comments I have ever read on the subject of controlling leisure time came from the late Greek billionaire Aristotle Onassis. He once said, "I have come to the conclusion that the way you get to be a celebrity is to get control of people's playthings. It's a little like children and their toys. You do not become a celebrity by controlling the people's money, their banks, their national resources, their raw materials. . . . If I had remained just a shipping man, I would have remained relatively obscure. But the moment I bought Monte Carlo, that was something else again. I then controlled one of the people's playthings. I was like a man who owned motion picture companies, or a television network, or a racetrack or horses or a ball team. They are all celebrities, and since I controlled the most famous casino in the world, I became one of the most famous men in the world."

By understanding the flamboyance of these types of men and by gathering every piece of information that you can obtain about the other side, you have a good chance of persuading anyone, at any level, to take one action or another.

I often think of Anwar Sadat and Menachem Begin's Camp David peace accords as one of history's great riddles. What was it that ultimately persuaded Sadat to have the courage and the boldness in the face of every cultural, political, and religious obstacle, to go forward in his peace initiative? I represented Sadat's daughter, Camelia, and she told me that her father asked to spend time with her before his visit to Camp David, because he told her he knew he would die at some point in time due to the results of his upcoming peace session.

Thus, the question echoes through time: what persuaded Sadat to do what he did? An event early in his life? A series of events? Was it the pressure or encouragement from people who were important to him? Was it his ego? Or all of these factors? What was the key that turned the lock to a centuries-old stalemate in the Middle East? No matter how small the scale, or how modest the stakes, *any* negotiation can be boiled down to the same idea: is there a key to the other person that will help you to dictate his response?

Whose Authority Is It?

Does your negotiating partner make his or her own decisions? You will save immeasurable time by discovering if you are dealing with the person who has the authority to say yes, or if they are misleading you about their role. If they do have the authority, are they the type who can make decisions? Donald Trump can madden you by listening to literally dozens of people before he arrives at an answer. Of course, based on his success, he must be talking to some of the right people, some of the time.

A man who could make decisions was Sonny Werblin. After Sonny sold the Jets, he became president of Madison Square Garden, which owned the New York Knicks. I visited Sonny one year at his home in Saratoga, New York, to work on center Bill Cartwright's first contract with the Knicks. I had spent months negotiating with the team's general manager, and had come to an impasse with him on some of the terms I was seeking for Bill's protection.

The Knicks had been burnt before on contracts carrying long guarantees and the general manager had refused to grant them to me. So I turned to Werblin, the man in charge. I wasn't disappointed when at the end of a ten-minute conversation Werblin said, "I will accommodate you on the guarantees if you work with me on the deferred compensation." That was it. He had made his own decisions and he had the authority to carry them through.

Who and What Influences Your Opponent?

If you are dealing with someone who must rely on another person's judgment, find out who that person is. This applies whether you are trying to work out a contract or selling a product. When I deal with an executive at a television network, I may come close to an agreement only to have it rejected by the president. Or they will play "good guy–bad guy" with me. This is a fascinating game that has some of the elements of a Broadway musical. The lyrics run along the lines of, "I want to do it, but this other guy won't let me." Normally, you never hear from the bad guy. You are always talking with the good guy, while the mysterious Mr. No is out walking his pet rat.

Is He Under Any Special Pressures?

In preparing to negotiate, I am just as careful in finding out the climate in which the other party is dealing as I am the issues we will be discussing. It is of tremendous benefit for me to know the pressures the other side will be working under. It's like a negative weather report. If I know he has a time restraint, I may stand more firm as the deadline approaches, knowing he would rather make further concessions than lose the deal altogether. If he is being publicly criticized for losing players to better offers from other teams, I may make one fewer concession than I otherwise would, aware that he would rather salvage his reputation than win that individual point.

In defining the pressures on the other side, information is the key to success. Often the desired information is extremely public. I read the daily papers from around the country to maintain a feel for the marketplace. If I am about to negotiate with the Los Angeles Rams, I make a point of reading the *Los Angeles Times* and the *Los Angeles Daily News* to find out what "X" is saying and what people are saying about him. Since I live in Boston, if I didn't make the effort to read the local papers in Los Angeles, I might not know that at a given moment, the Rams have been saddled with a string of injuries and management is under fire for contracting fragile athletes. If my client, for example, is a workhorse who has never missed a game in his seven-year career, I will now know of an added strength which I wouldn't have known about if I hadn't done my research.

In Seattle, the Supersonics may have lost more basketball games than expected and there may be a newspaper poll inciting the team to fire the general manager. If so, that general manager will be in a different mood and bargaining position than if he were being portrayed in the press as the beleaguered general manager trying to do his best. Clearly, I would lose a golden opportunity if I did not make it my business to accumulate this information and use it to my client's benefit.

While most businesses are not as highly visible as professional sports, industry newsletters and trade papers serve the same function in their fields that the dailies serve in mine. It is best to be on top of the news that is pertinent to your field of endeavor. Establishing a network of confidants is also valuable. Everyone has a community, and few people are so isolated that they can't be influenced by the people around them. If a boss is up for promotion and needs an assistant, know about it. If profits are down and the section must produce or be reorganized, be on top of it. Does everybody love the new office manager? Nobody? There is always news traveling on the wire, whether it is the Associated Press or the telephone. Make every effort to tap into it.

Whose Money Is He Spending?

Few pieces of information are more vital than knowing if you are meeting with someone who is spending OPM—Other People's Money— or his own. The reasons are obvious. If you are talking to Jack Diller or Al Bianchi for a deal with the New York Knicks, which are owned by the multibillion-dollar Paramount Communications Inc., you will be dealing more with pure business attitudes and considerations. Diller and Bianchi are there to do business. They're secure. A wrong decision is tax-deductible. A series of wrong decisions may cost them their jobs, but not their life savings.

These are people with whom I can speak freely about dollars as opposed to, say, former New England Patriots owner Billy Sullivan, who was spending his own money. While it's tough to generalize, usually when someone's negotiations involve his or her own money, those negotiations will proceed at a slower pace.

Set Your Goals

You've now prepared yourself in market value, knowing your client, yourself, and your adversary. The information-gathering part of your job may be done, but now it's time for the pre-negotiation drill. In one sense, you'll be doing a dry run before the real thing.

You should start by setting your goals. You want to spend $15,000 for a new car or you want a $50,000 salary. Or you're willing to go as high as $450,000 for the house of your dreams. Be aware that these goals are pre-negotiation estimates. Like many other estimates, they are expected to change. For your sake, you want them to change to your advantage, but you must be prepared to revise upward or downward if need be, but even then, to a limit. You should keep reassessing your goals as you negotiate so that you continue to ask or expect something that is realistic and not impossible to attain.

Sometimes, it is helpful to delineate the levels of satisfaction before the negotiation. For instance, on a scale of 1 to 100, you would be thrilled with 100, happy with 75, satisfied with 50, disappointed with 25, and mortified with 0.

Preparing Your Argument: the Positive Side

Ideally, the argument you will present to convince the other side of your position should be a positive one. You will want to present yourself or your client in the best light possible and your presentation will be compelling enough to make your negotiating partner agree to most or all of your requests.

A lawyer believes he has worked long hours, done superlative work, and contributed to the burgeoning reputation and financial success of his fast-growing law firm. He believes he deserves at the least a substantial raise, and at the most, an offer of partnership. He hasn't been denied the spoils he thinks he has earned, nor have they been offered. Look at this as an example:

"Mr. Gardner, as you know I've handled every assignment you've given me, and you've frequently complimented my work, both in person and in notes. I took on work that other, more senior lawyers didn't want to do, did it quickly and completely, and opened up a new line of practice for us with the promise of an added and lucrative clientele. More clientele means more billings for the firm, which I believe I should get a share in.

"You have no idea how much I enjoy the work I'm doing here and how much I appreciate the opportunities you've given me to advance myself. It's the most exhilarating work I've done since I passed the bar. I know that other lawyers with the same experience I have are earning more than I am. Some of them are also partners. I think when you analyze the work I've done that I merit the same treatment as my colleagues."

Notice there isn't a "demand" in the presentation. The lawyer isn't trying to force his boss's hand, threatening to leave, or balking at taking on more work if his demands aren't met. He's presenting his case calmly and clearly. Most importantly, he is being reasonable by seeking a raise or a partnership, putting both thoughts in his supervisor's mind, rather than just one.

Preparing Your Argument: the Negative Side

Often, a persuasive argument can be made not so much *for* your position as for its being the best of a series of less attractive options. If you can catalog, one-by-one, all the unpleasant situations which could possibly occur, and make the other side understand that your deal is the best available, they may accept it even if the terms are not particularly to their liking. The lesser of two evils may still be evil, but it's preferable to getting *really* stuck.

An account executive at an advertising agency feels he has earned a raise which management has thus far denied him. He wants to stay with the firm but knows he must get the attention of his superiors with the seriousness of his request.

He may go to his boss and say, "Mr. Carlyle, I would like to request a raise in my salary. I believe the quality of my work merits this increase. I don't want to go elsewhere but I am afraid that I really do need this increase. If it were necessary for me to go elsewhere, and for my place to be filled by a new employee, the company would first have to find a qualified replacement. This is a time-consuming process which would saddle the company with costly down time while the search was being conducted and the decision made.

"Training the new person would also create a negative cash flow because none of the business which comes out of that office could be brought forth while the new position was being brought up to speed. This is a smooth-running office. This break-in period will cost the company not only in terms of productivity, but with respect to worker interactions. And, where you have always praised the quality of my work, it is also possible that a new person in my position might not perform as consistently to your high standards.

"Finally, if the person you find to replace me doesn't work out, the company will be forced to go through the entire difficult replacement process all over again, with the same potentially negative consequences and an increased possibility of damaged office morale. This entire scenario can be prevented if you will only consider favorably my request for a raise. I feel I deserve it. And not only will you eliminate all of these unfortunate, costly, but quite foreseeable possibilities, but by rewarding me you will guarantee having an even more enthusiastic and productive worker on your team. *Both* of us will benefit."

If the amount of the request is within reason, there is every chance that this line of persuasion will be successful.

Preparing for Vinny Testaverde

Now that I have taken you through the steps of proper preparation, let me show you how I have used this approach so many times in my own work. For example, my preparation to negotiate on behalf of University of Miami quarterback Vinny Testaverde told me I had a rare commodity: he was handsome, wholesome, and extremely talented, perfect for the Tampa Bay Buccaneers, a perennial doormat in the National Football League, the team that had made Vinny the number one selection in the 1987 college draft.

But facing me was one of the most formidable owners in professional sports: banker and real estate developer Hugh Culverhouse, a former commissioner of the Internal Revenue Service, with a personal fortune of more than $350 million.

Since hearing from Vinny's dad, Al Testaverde, in late 1985, I had been keeping a file on the young man. And in late 1986, when I was asked to represent Vinny, I began to study it. I also did a little leg work: I spoke with a raft of scouts, general managers, and owners to get as candid a range of opinion as possible about Vinny's talent. I do this with virtually every player I represent. I make it a point not to rely on hearsay or my own inexpert judgments.

The verdict on Vinny was unanimous: this was a franchise player, maybe the best quarterback to come out of college since Joe Namath, and judged ahead of star NFL quarterbacks Jim Kelly and Dan Marino at comparative points in their careers. Not bad. His glowing on- and off-the-field credentials from nearly everyone were like the long litany of superlatives I'd heard about Larry Bird.

My Testaverde preparation found this:

- If his value was similar to Jim Kelly's and Dan Marino's, then I surmised that he should be paid similarly. Kelly made $8 million over five years, while Marino was earning $9 million over six years. These were high salaries, I knew, but Vinny's talent, penchant for clean living, and potential to lead the Bucs out of desperate straits, made paying him at that level a viable request. Whether Culverhouse would agree with me was another question, but it was my starting point, and I felt justified and comfortable with it.

Sure, paying Vinny that much didn't make total sense. He'd never played in the pros, but my research showed me that this was an exploitable market, with a foundation built on a rich lode of potential. The agents and players hadn't created this market. The owners had. A person or product is worth what the market will bear, what just one person is willing to pay.

So I entered my talks with Culverhouse with copies of the contracts of Kelly, Marino, Bernie Kosar, and Joe Montana. I knew that with Vinny I had a virtual goodwill ambassador; he didn't smoke, drank little, and had a very close relationship with his family. Vinny's success as a player was a dream come true for his emotionally charged father, Al, who broke down tearfully on the night his son accepted the Heisman Trophy. They always kissed when they saw each other, which told me something about the family's values. This was a good kid from a good family. Vinny also loved Florida and would be perfect, professionally and personally, for hero-starved Tampa Bay fans. Vinny was a solid player and a solid citizen who would cause no problems. He could only help the Buc's flagging image.

- I had researched Hugh Culverhouse in *Who's Who In America*, the *Forbes* 400, *Fortune*, and any periodical I could find with an article about him. He was enormously wealthy, much of it earned in real estate and banking. He was considered a savvy lawyer whose clients had included Richard Nixon. At sixty-seven, he was adventurous; he was known to fly his own airplane for overnight jaunts to South Korea or Paris.

Though he had a previous reputation for being close with a dollar, it was significant that he just opened his wallet to sign Ray Perkins as head coach for $800,000 a year. This piece of information told me that Culverhouse wanted a winner badly and was willing to pay for one. After all, Culverhouse had endured two embarrassing 2–14 seasons in a row. He had also drafted the multitalented Bo Jackson (who now plays baseball with the Kansas City Royals and football with the Los Angeles Raiders) in the first round of the draft the previous year, but Jackson didn't sign with the Bucs. Instead, he played baseball that year.

Even though it was obvious that Culverhouse wanted to recover from the loss of a great athlete like Jackson by signing another franchise player like Vinny Testaverde, he was under great pressure in his position as chairman of the NFL's Management Council, the NFL owners' ruling body. In that role, he was charged with holding salaries down and restricting player movement. Paying Vinny Jim Kelly–sized dollars certainly held the potential of souring his relationship with the more hard-line owners. Which way would he go?

I knew Vinny could help salvage the team's sagging business side. The team drew meager crowds at that time. By filling up only half of its seats during the 1986 season, the total lost revenues—based on an average ticket price of about $14 and the team's cuts of concession and parking income—amounted to $4 million. I reasoned that if the Bucs spruced up its team, management could fill the stadium and raise the price of tickets and luxury box rentals, producing an increased cash flow that would more than make up for the size of Vinny's salary.

I was accentuating Vinny's considerable assets and probing Culverhouse's weak spots. If I could convince Culverhouse that signing Vinny would help the team win and burnish Culverhouse's tarnished image as a sportsman, then my job would be complete. Once I'd figured out Culverhouse's vulnerabilities, I didn't say, "Hugh, if you don't give Vinny the money he deserves, we're going to walk away like Bo did, and you will be a laughingstock again." I played subtly on his deep concerns and civic ego. But I didn't trample on them.

Over the course of several months of negotiations Culverhouse finally agreed with my view of the situation and Vinny signed an $8.2 million contract over six years. Even though it was more money than Culverhouse had ever paid for a player or guaranteed, there were no angry feelings, nor has he ever expressed regret to me about paying Vinny's asking price.

CHAPTER FOUR

Preparation on an International Level

"Let our advance worrying become advance thinking and planning."

—SIR WINSTON CHURCHILL

"It is no use to wait for your ship to come in unless you have sent one out."

—BELGIAN PROVERB

IF YOU'VE traveled abroad, you know how tough getting around can be if you don't know the local language and customs. Asking for street directions or the location of your hotel can be frustrating if you don't know how to properly make your desires known. Everybody's heard about the American tourist in Paris who thinks he is making himself understood by speaking English a little more loudly than he would at home. Then he gets upset when he is unable to make his intentions clear.

Such disappointments can certainly be avoided with just a little home-work.

Trying to do business internationally without knowing a country's language and style of doing business or its people's social customs, morals, and body language is almost a certain journey to failure. Taking a trip armed only with the description of your product and the price you want for it is just not enough in this world of international interaction. Every bit of work you've done can go up in smoke if you say or do the wrong thing, even if you don't mean it.

Because entertainment and sports have become global interests, I have negotiated in and traveled throughout countries such as Japan, England, France, West Germany, Sweden, Italy, Australia, Finland, the Soviet Union, Israel, Spain, Canada, and Mexico. I'm still learning the finer points of the customs, the styles, and the correct protocols of those foreign lands. Many of the precepts I've been discussing have been learned the hard way. Take what happened to me one evening in Egypt, for instance.

During a trip to the Middle East, Camelia Sadat, daughter of the late Egyptian president, Anwar Sadat, invited me for dinner at her mother's home in Cairo. I am Camelia's counsel and had negotiated her publishing contract for a biography of her father. We met to discuss some terms of the deal at her family's home. I was pleased and flattered that she asked me to meet her extended family.

Seated around the large dinner table were twenty members of the Sadat family, including his first wife and his daughters Rokaya, Rawia, and Camelia in addition to me and my wife, Anne. Some of the relatives had traveled a long way from Sadat's home village of Mit Abul-Kum. The Sadats are a talkative, enthusiastic family. We spent a festive and entertaining evening with them. I've always admired Sadat, and during the evening, I was able to ask questions about Sadat's young life, his political career, and what motivated him to negotiate peace accords with Israel in 1979.

After dessert, one of Camelia's relatives leaned toward me and asked, "Bob, did you enjoy the meal?"

94

I smiled and said, "Oh, perfect," and made the O.K. sign, forming a circle with my thumb and forefinger. Was that ever a mistake! Several people shrieked. Others just stared at me with looks of absolute horror written on their faces. I was shocked. What had I done? That's what I always do to signify okay, innocently thinking that the symbol translated across countries and cultures.

To my relief, I heard Camelia laugh. Camelia, who lives in the United States part-time and knows the meanings of American gestures, said, "Bob, that okay sign is probably the most obscene gesture you can make in Egypt."

She explained it all to her family, and they laughed heartily and quickly forgave me. But I shudder to think what the reaction would be if I flashed that sign at the end of an important negotiation in Egypt. I'm not so sure my host would be so forgiving.

I'm not ashamed to admit that I've made a few mistakes when I've traveled abroad—thankfully none that damaged my clients' interests or caused an international incident. But these faux pas remind me again just how much I need to prepare myself beyond the details of my negotiation, always remembering to seek a lot of help from local experts to smooth my way.

My need to know the fundamentals of foreign deal-making is more crucial than ever because of the internationalization of business. Barriers are falling every day to create a global marketplace. Faxes, telexes, computers and state-of-the-art telephone technologies have speeded up the pace of communications and information, making the world ever smaller.

More joint ventures are being signed between American companies and foreign countries. American-based cable TV companies are wiring Hong Kong, Denmark, England, Ireland, Israel and France. In 1992 the European Common Market will link its members into one economic powerhouse, making knowledge about global negotiating more important than ever.

In the sports world, the pace of internationalization is picking up. The National Football League has already created a new international league, called the World League of American Football, which will start playing in the spring of 1991 with four teams in Western Europe. NFL exhibitions in England have packed Wembley Stadium since 1986, spawning the growth of amateur and semipro American-style football teams throughout the country.

Nothing better illustrates the growth of basketball globally than the signing of Duke University star center Danny Ferry, the number-two pick in the 1989 National Basketball Association draft, to a $2 million per year contract with an Italian team, instead of with the Los Angeles Clippers in the NBA. From Spain and France to Italy and Israel, pro basketball has become the national obsession, and the thirst for NBA-level play is seen in the rabid interest paid to NBA exhibitions and the year-round sales of more than $50 million in licensed NBA merchandise.

While Major League Baseball isn't contemplating foreign expansion, it is experiencing growing popularity abroad on television, where baseball is reaping record revenues. Japan now signs American players in the prime, not decline, of their careers, like former Atlanta Brave Bob Horner, for whom the Yakult Swallows paid $2 million in 1987. Additional interest around the world is growing as the 1992 Summer Olympics approach and baseball becomes a medal sport for the first time.

Hockey has for many years had a strong international flavor. National Hockey League teams have long played exhibitions in Europe and all-star teams have played in the Soviet Union. And, after many years of signing players from Sweden and Finland to play in the NHL, Soviet stars are now playing in the league; a goal that took years of tense negotiations with notoriously suspicious Soviet officials.

I have to be extremely patient when I'm negotiating abroad. So much is new and different. Every country has a different way of doing business that is tied to its history and culture. Most countries have a different pace of business than the United States does. American businessmen must understand that their counterparts in Madrid take an afternoon siesta. Get used to it. We can't expect everybody to be like us, even if we'd like it that way.

Because of their economic power, we often deal with the Japanese. But nobody has said it is easy. The path to an agreement with them can be slow and frustrating. Some years ago, I received requests to have Carl Yastrzemski film a TV commercial in Japan and promote a Japanese product. The prospect was intriguing because Yaz, then the star left fielder for the Boston Red Sox and now a Hall of Famer, had been singled out as a big superstar to sell a product only in Japan, only for Japanese consumers. So Carl and I and our wives, Carol and Anne, flew to Hawaii, and then to Japan. To preserve Yaz's privacy, he registered at the Imperial Hotel under an assumed name, Herman Matsui, the name of our host for the trip.

Although the hints were dropped only cryptically by the typically subtle Japanese, we sensed that we were headed for something bigger and more substantial than a commercial agreement. The first night, we dined with Takeo Koyama, owner of the Nagoya Chunichi Dragons, and his general manager, Wally Yonamine. We tried to eat privately, but news of our presence spread quickly, and group pictures of us in deep conversation appeared on the front pages of the leading newspapers in Tokyo the next day. Quickly, the papers in Boston picked it up. We hadn't talked business and already the story that Yaz was leaving for Japan was spreading fast. In Japan, Carl was already being recognized by the fans wherever he went—fans who greeted him with cheers of "Meester Yizminsky, Meester Yizminsky!"

With each passing day, Carl and Carol were starting to love Japan. They loved the courtesy, humility, and polite manners of the people, and began to think that if Koyama made the right offer, Yaz would at least consider playing there. Carl's interest was aroused further by Koyama's invitation for us to be his guests at his home in Nagoya, a four-hour train ride from Tokyo. No negotiations were held, but I had to explain our presence in the city. So I told reporters that we were on a sightseeing trip, to purchase some of the beautiful pottery the city was known for. I declared unfounded any reports that Yaz was signed.

When we returned to Tokyo, the phone rang in my hotel room and a voice said, "Hold line for Koyama-san, please." Koyama, who had by this time been advised against signing Yaz by the United States Commissioner of Baseball, was asking for a meeting to discuss a possible contract for Yastrzemski.

Koyama, a small, delicate man, arrived in disguise, wearing a surgical mask the Japanese use to guard against others suffering from colds, and his hat pulled over his eyes. We met in strict security in the Tokyo office of the Massachusetts Port Authority.

I had told Koyama during our first dinner that if Yaz would even consider coming to Japan, he would require a contract of $1 million over four years, with all his taxes and living expenses paid by the team. This is where the negotiating became quintessentially Japanese. I requested $1 million, an unprecedented figure at that time for a Japanese team to pay an American player. When I said, "One million," they nodded. They said "*Hai!*" They smiled. They didn't seem to be saying no. In fact, they seemed to be saying yes, even if they really weren't.

That's one of the aspects of the Japanese negotiating style that everybody encounters: the Japanese prize harmony and they don't want to seem disagreeable, even if they disagree. They're never overbearing and are always unfailingly polite.

When Japanese negotiators nod and smile, they are only trying to be polite and agreeable. They want to keep the talks amicable. When they say, "*Hai,*" they are being ambiguous. *Hai* roughly means, "Yes, I understand what you're saying." Although they may nod when they say it, in no way does it mean they have agreed to anything. It's very easy to be misled by their penchant for agreeability.

Koyama countered with $150,000, still below what we felt the Red Sox would offer, even if the American salary would suffer from the taxes Yaz would have to pay. In three more meetings, punctuated by a lot of bowing and nods of the head, neither of us budged from our positions. Koyama said that he would present our numbers to his board of directors. Talks continued by telephone between Boston and Tokyo, ending with Koyama's final offer of $175,000 after taxes, with a free apartment and car. When the negotiations ended, however, Yaz decided to stay with the Red Sox in deference to his deep affection for Red Sox owner Tom Yawkey.

Dealing with the Japanese hasn't changed in the years since. They are still deliberate and courteous and, well, inscrutable. But as usual, in doing business abroad, you cannot assume that their behavior and business customs will mimic those of an American.

In the summer of 1989, I returned to Tokyo with San Francisco 49ers quarterback Joe Montana, who had led his team earlier that year to its second Super Bowl victory. Joe was immensely popular in Japan, and as the hero of that year's Super Bowl, he then held a special appeal. So he had been invited to attend the Super Bowl of Japan and videotape a commercial for Toshiba.

Joe's contract with Toshiba had been negotiated separately by the 49ers, but I had also agreed to its terms. When I saw the agreement for $300,000, I thought it was fine. But I was in for a big surprise. When I was talking to Toshiba officials in Tokyo, they informed me that the terms of their contracts didn't run in years, but in quarters, with possible renewal. So Joe wasn't going to earn $300,000 for the year, potentially he was going to make $1,000,000! I had assumed that they negotiated by the year. Thankfully the miscalculation worked in Joe's favor.

There is almost no way you can negotiate internationally without some misunderstandings. It's natural. But if you plan in advance, read about the countries you're traveling to, and talk to colleagues about their experiences abroad, you can minimize your surprises. Now I know that Asians use middlemen for some aspects of their negotiating to minimize direct conflict. Chinese dislike hearty backslapping and are very punctual, and they expect you to show patience while they make a decision.

The Turkish people are deeply offended if you clench your fist and point your thumb skyward in the sign of the hitchhiker, even though Brazilians view it as a symbol of good luck. The English deem it obscene if you make the familiar V-for-victory sign and turn your palm toward yourself. Japanese should never be put in a position where they will lose face or have to admit failure, and Koreans don't feel contract provisions are written in concrete, even if they're written into the contract.

Indonesians make decisions very slowly because their concept of time is different from ours. Soviets are usually expressionless during talks and they will delay and bargain, while Arabs are emotional and volatile, and will trust you more if you vigorously haggle for the best price.

In addition to being wary of doing or saying the wrong thing, it's a good idea to be considerate with your hosts in order to create the right atmosphere. Whenever I travel, I try to learn a few basic expressions in the native language, like "Hello," "Good-bye," "Thank you," and "How are you?" It shows that you are making an effort to learn the ways of those with whom you hope to deal.

Even as a tourist, you can take note of the way foreigners will negotiate. Just walk into an Arab bazaar. People are shouting so much you'd think that they're arguing. But there they are, standing closer to each other than Americans would in a similar situation, loudly proclaiming their positions. But they're just bargaining. That's their style.

Every culture seems to have a tradition that forms the style of negotiations there. Soviet-American arms negotiations are often punctuated by walk-outs and apparent huffs. The Soviets are notorious for delays and precipitous presentations of new conditions. Not that the Americans aren't difficult in their own peculiar way, but the Soviets have an exceptional reputation.

I'll never forget one of my first negotiating experiences in the U.S.S.R. It was back in the 1970s and I was headed to Moscow for the hockey series between Team Canada and the Soviet team. I was also going to do a favor for John "Misha" Petkevich, then the North American figure skating champion and a student at Harvard. He asked me if I could gain the Soviet government's go-ahead for their top figure skaters to travel to the United States. An exhibition tour, featuring American and Soviet stars, was to be arranged with the proceeds going to charity.

This was during the early days of détente with the Soviet Union, and the Cold War seemed to be cooling. The People's Republic of China was beginning to open itself to the West, and President Nixon had made his historic visit there. So I was optimistic, but naturally cautious.

In Moscow, I headed for the U.S. consulate to explain the nature of my trip. The officials asked what my approach to the Soviets would be when I met with the head of the Soviet Figure Skating Federation. Confidently, I said, "I'll explain that their skaters would be given nothing but the best. Everywhere they went and everything they did would be first class. We'd make sure that they would not lack for anything."

Again, I was naive. This wasn't what you told an official in the Soviet Union. The consular officials grinned at each other, as if I'd said something funny. One of them clued me in. "Bob, if you tell them that, not one figure skater will be allowed to set foot outside Russia. They don't want their people to be treated first class. They don't want them to have anything in the way of courtesies or comforts. If you told them you were going to give them nothing, show them nothing, they'd be happy. Because that's how it is here. No one is a star. Everyone is treated the same. No one has first-class treatment."

I was stunned, but the information was useful. When I met the federation's leader, I assured him that the skaters would be treated as the Soviet government wanted them to be treated. These negotiations laid the foundation for a later trip by the Soviets to the United States.

Although Soviet leader Mikhail Gorbachev has invigorated his country through the openness of *glasnost* and tried to shake up its stagnant economy via *perestroika*, I don't think things have changed all that much. While there is a trickle of Soviet stars performing in the United States and other countries, most Soviet athletes generally retire to quiet lives of coaching, not million-dollar TV commercials or first-class Western-style treatment.

While the Soviets are usually unyielding and unemotional negotiators, the Italians are the opposite. They love to bargain, not as a tactical maneuver to delay an agreement, but as a productive and natural part of the whole process. Some years ago, I visited Italy to negotiate a contract for Boston College forward Terry Driscoll, who had been chosen in the first round of the NBA draft by the Detroit Pistons. Terry wasn't happy with the prospect of playing for Detroit, then one of the worst teams in the league, and our trip to Bologna was something of a lark. The Bologna team, like all Italian teams, was sponsored by major companies. But it was classified as an *amateur* team.

We were treated royally there. An American player was an automatic star on an Italian team, and the handsome Driscoll quickly became the charismatic *Driscolloni*, Big Driscoll. The Bolognese believed Terry was something extraordinary.

Our first negotiating session was not to be believed, yet it was typically Italian. The team official and I met in a hotel room, and our negotiating was unlike anything I've ever experienced. It was loud. It was menacing. It was downright scary. My wife, Anne, who was in a nearby room, thought we had come to blows. But this was merely a spirited arena for my hosts. Shouting, yelling, and gesticulating comprised their style. They didn't behave this way because they were angry or dismayed by our asking price. That's just the way they were. Even if it sounded like they didn't want anything to do with us, they kept upping their figures, and we were amazed at their intensity. Our talks still sounded more like a violent argument, but we played along.

Terry put pressure on them by playing a brief but spectacular few minutes for a team in a coastal resort town of Riccione. He was like Michael Jordan, Magic Johnson, and Larry Bird all wrapped up in one. I didn't want Terry to hurt himself, so after his short stint, I insisted that Terry leave the court.

What we wanted from the team was a salary equivalent to an NBA superstar's. Six years of medical school, free. A rent-free apartment for a year. And a new Maserati. All for just twenty-two games, to be played once a week, every Sunday. The Italians agreed to it, much to our surprise. But they wanted Terry to sign. Immediately. Sign it *now*, they said insistently. Again, the Italian style. Terry only had to sign his name and he'd have a dream package. But I wanted to think about it more. I wanted Terry to think about it. So I made a few calls back to the United States, one of them to Red Auerbach at his home in Washington, D.C.

"Red," I said, "this is Bob Woolf. I'm calling from Bologna."

"That's where you belong, Woolf, in Bologna," Red said, in his gruff way. When he heard the Italian offer, he said quickly, "Bob, Terry has to take it. He'd be crazy to turn down a deal like that."

Then I told our hosts that we needed more time and I took Terry and my wife to London. Once we got there, Terry decided on Italy. "I'll never get a chance like this in my life," he said. "If I don't like it, I can always go back to the NBA next year."

Terry played that season in Italy, and returned to the NBA the next year for a productive, professional career. Ironically, when his NBA days were over, *Driscolloni* returned to Bologna to play and coach there.

Never underestimate your need for expert help in foreign countries. Translators, lawyers, and tax experts top my list of crucial middlemen. Not only is the language different in most countries, but the maze of strange criminal, civil, and tax laws can drive you crazy if you negotiate them blindly.

A few tips on translators. Remember, when you're negotiating, translators are your sole means for verbal communication. Make them a partner, an ally. If you have time, brief them in advance of your negotiations so they understand what you'll be saying. Speak slowly and steer clear of slang and strange words. Speak in short and concise sentences, and avoid long stretches of back-and-forth translation. And be sure to let the interpreter rest after a few hours.

When I was in Israel with an American all-star team I had brought there to play a series of exhibition games with Israeli stars, I wish I had had an interpreter on hand even though English *is* spoken side-by-side with Hebrew. Among the players on the team were Larry Bird, Calvin Murphy, Pat Cummings, and Billy Paultz. We played games in

Tel Aviv, Haifa, and Jerusalem. In my negotiations with the Israelis, I made sure that when we played in Jerusalem, it would be in an air-conditioned building. When we got there, and I asked for the air conditioner to be turned on, all I got was a workman opening a window on the roof. I should have gotten a better definition of "air conditioning."

You have to be aware of all the terms outlined in every contract wherever you travel. In subsequent negotiations in Israel, I've hired local translators and attorneys to help me with contracts, which are written in Hebrew and then translated into English. I don't speak Hebrew at all, so I have to rely on a faithful translation into English to be sure that everybody agrees on all conditions—and what they mean.

On that Israeli tour, the desert heat was tough on all of us. We needed all the air conditioning and heat relief we could get. One day, on the team bus to Jerusalem, Larry Bird got sick. He looked terrible and it seemed to me that he was about to faint. So I immediately took him off the bus and into a hotel room and told the team to see the sights in Bethlehem and Jerusalem.

I called a doctor, who came quickly. "He's terribly dehydrated," said the doctor, "so you have to feed him as much liquids as possible. I don't care if you have to keep waking him up, just keep feeding him liquids."

"Do you think he can play tonight?" I asked.

The doctor held up a tall glass. "If he can fill this glass by tonight then he can play," said the doctor.

I woke Larry up periodically and gave him every liquid I could find—orange juice, soda, milk, and water. By around four in the afternoon, Larry said, "I feel better. Do you think I can play tonight?"

"Larry, the doctor said you can play only if you fill up this glass," I told him.

"Thank God it's you, Mr. Woolf," said Larry. "If that were Red Auerbach, he would have brought in a *thimble*."

* * *

If you are lacking information on international procedures, it is necessary to seek out and rely on responsible local experts. I've never seen a situation quite like the recording group, the New Kids on the Block. These five clean-cut teenaged boys from Boston have chalked up hit after hit with their funky sound. I've never represented anybody whose popularity and earning power has exploded in so short a time as the New Kids. Their most recent album went multi-platinum, selling over eight million copies. They received over 400,000 calls a month on their "900" phone line, and broke all existing records for licensing and merchandising sales.

Acting as their business manager has been fascinating. Planning to send them on a world tour isn't a matter of putting them on a plane and wishing them good luck. When Jerry Ade, their booking agent, set up their tour, which included dates in Japan, Australia, Singapore, Manila, and Western Europe, he called upon tax and financial experts to minimize the New Kids' tax liability, which varies widely in each country, and to negotiate payment only in U.S. dollars to avoid fluctuations in the local currency's exchange rate. Usually, payment is made through a bank wire to the United States. But sometimes it's not so easy and the promoters have to find other ways to properly transfer the money to the New Kids' account.

Dick Scott, the New Kids' personal manager, hired middlemen and informed experts in each country to gauge what size arenas and stadiums the Kids could fill and to track how frequently the group's records were being played to determine the correct amounts of foreign royalties.

You need to know details such as the Japanese government's requirement that a touring musician or group get a letter of invitation from the U.S. State Department. If they don't, no visa will be granted and hence no performance. In this type of situation, you need to be aware of the need to hire people who know what you don't in international procedures. Proper preparation doesn't always mean learning and handling everything yourself.

Having clients in potentially dangerous situations abroad alerts you to changes you have to make in your requests during negotiations. When I represented NBC News correspondent Bonnie Anderson, she had just transferred from the Rome bureau to Beirut, the middle of one of the most perilous places on earth. The civil war between the Christians and Moslems was in full force. So I wouldn't have been doing my job if I didn't do my utmost to minimize the danger Bonnie was in by negotiating clauses in her agreement that would never appear in a domestic media contract.

Under the terms of her contract, NBC purchased a generator for her apartment in case her building got bombed and lost power; gave her a new medical policy in case she was shot, injured or killed in the course of a story; and a leave policy that provided her with three days off in Rome for every sixteen days she worked in Beirut. NBC agreed to all the terms with little argument. They were aware it was a difficult situation. One year later, NBC evacuated their correspondents from Beirut, citing the peril in staying any longer. Always be sure to consider the particular situations that can be created because of the locale, customs, or history (past or current) of a certain foreign country.

I would much rather be over-prepared for an international business or social encounter rather than be embarrassed. In 1989, Armand Hammer invited me and my wife to join a group who would be visiting Prince Charles and Princess Diana in England. As you can imagine, I was most anxious to properly prepare for meeting royalty. What was the correct way to address them? Was there any particular protocol to follow? What was the proper attire for a royal reception or the polo match that we would be attending? As it turned out, Prince Charles and Princess Diana treated us with such warmth and openness that the expected formality was brushed aside almost immediately. We then embarked on a weekend full of laughter, with private jokes and even a dance with Princess Di. Even though Prince Charles excelled in his polo match, he confided in me that he was probably a little too old to become a member of the professional circuit. I told him, "Don't worry, we'll create a seniors' circuit!" The Prince promised to call me if he ever decides to join the seniors' circuit and we all left that weekend feeling as if we'd attended a family outing.

As the above would indicate, I was pleasantly surprised that my apprehension about protocol turned out to be unwarranted. However, once again, it's always a good idea to go into any situation totally prepared.

CHAPTER FIVE

Style

"Style is effectiveness of assertion."

—GEORGE BERNARD SHAW

"The real art of conversation is not only to say the right thing in the right place but to leave unsaid the wrong thing at the tempting moment."

—BENJAMIN FRANKLIN

"Whether it is strikes or war, even the biggest battles in history have ended sitting down at a table. What is better—to be a boxing champion or a chess champion? I prefer chess."

—LECH WALESA

IT'S NOT yet enough that you've fine-tuned the atmosphere and researched your case, yourself, and your client. You still have a necessary step to consider before you are ready to begin.

It's called style.

Style has nothing to do with an expensive Giorgio Armani double-breasted suit or a Donna Karan dress. Instead, I'm talking about the personal statement your actions make to other people. Style is a crucial aspect of your dealings; it is not what you do, but how you do it and how you express something. Style is how you speak and how you listen; how you look at someone and how you appear; how you keep your anger under wraps and your ego in check.

The essence of style is in making the other side feel comfortable and persuadable. If you can remove another person's anxieties about the process, about yourself, and about what you want, you've taken a major step toward success. A good teacher or good motivator exudes quiet self-confidence, reduces others' fears and makes them feel good about themselves. A good negotiator does the same thing. "It doesn't hurt to ask" is one of my negotiation credos. But when it comes to style, it's how you ask that matters.

Keep "Demand" Out of Your Vocabulary

When I am talking to someone, I try to choose my words very carefully so as not to offend someone or alienate them in the course of a conversation. When I am negotiating, I never make demands. I never lay down ultimatums. The word "demand" is not in my vocabulary. I don't even like the word. I don't use it and find it offensive when others use it.

If someone marched into my office with their list of demands, I'd want to show them the way out, wouldn't you? This is the kind of aggressive, intimidating language that will kill ninety-nine deals out of a hundred. Nobody wants to hear that brand of tough talk, nor are they likely to accommodate you if placed unpleasantly under the gun.

The aim of a negotiation is to arrive at an acceptable conclusion, not just to prove your prowess. Think bottom line: will someone react more favorably when he is threatened or when he is treated with verbal respect? Will he soften his stance or will his opposition stiffen? In order to work *with* and not against someone, it is best to use language in its least offending form.

When I want to let the other side know my goals in a negotiation, instead of making demands, I make *suggestions*, I make *recommendations*, I make *proposals*. "May I suggest this?" is so much more graceful than "This is what I want." And when you are negotiating, it is exactly the same thing. "Could you live with this?" "Does this make sense?" "Is this all right with you?" "Is this outlandish?" "Is this crazy?" are all preferable to, "These are my demands, I won't take a penny less." Or "You'd better accept this because it's as far as I'm going."

The success of your negotiating technique will depend in large part on the way it is presented. To demonstrate that you hold your negotiating partner in respect, you should show all the dignity that language can confer. Don't say, "I want you to hear my pitch." How much more genteel and effective it is to say, "I would like you to hear my presentation." Note the difference in style: the latter is more formal and presents no demand.

I never say, "Take it or leave it." Many negotiators, when backed into that corner, will "leave it" on principle rather than be bullied. Sometimes even if the terms are acceptable, the attitude is not.

If I have come to what is my final position, I will most likely say, "I hope you understand, this is the best I can do. I hope we will be able to work together." The point is the same, my position is unchanged, but in one case the opposition is being challenged, while in the other it is being asked for a rational appraisal.

Who, in that situation, would not prefer to be treated amiably and not respond in kind? Assuming the other side understands that your stand is firm, a shouted "Absolutely not!" is simply an inferior response to a calmly stated "I'm afraid we have a problem in that area."

I've seen many negotiations when one person will say, "That offer is an insult." In my mind, there is hardly any offer that is an insult. The offer may not be competitive. It may not be what you wanted. But rarely is anyone trying to insult you. In many cases, the buyer wants to offer as little as possible and is prepared to go higher. Rather than say you're insulted by a low offer, you're better off saying, "That wasn't what I had in mind."

Often in a negotiation, you use timing as a way of getting things moving. Even then there is a more and less effective way of stating your position. "This is on the table until Friday at four o'clock" is a crude attempt to create a crisis and a hurried mentality which will force the other side into movement. I have found it better to say, "Because of outside influences, unfortunately, I have a time restraint problem; I can allow that proposal to be honored only until four o'clock on Friday."

The two statements clearly mean the same thing but the effects are entirely different. In the first instance, I am a hard-nose who doesn't care about anything but myself; while in the second, I am a man who wants to work with the other side, but is slightly restrained and hopes to be accommodated. It feels better to work with the second person. What's more, it feels better to *be* the second person.

Type of Language

Always keep your language polite. There is no place for rough, profane language in a negotiation. The last thing you want is for someone to think of you as vulgar, with no distinguishing refinement. Even if the person with whom you are negotiating is impolite, don't follow his lead. Be dignified. Eventually, the other side will rise to your level. Your words and your bearing will make a statement: "I am a gentleman/lady and assume you are as well. I will not let these talks slip into the gutter."

How do you respond to profanity from the other side of the table? Just restrain yourself. Don't appear shocked or disapproving. You don't want to make the other person feel uncomfortable. And if your opponent doesn't raise the level of his discourse, keep your eyes on the prize; don't change your demeanor to accommodate a less preferable level of behavior.

Tone of Voice

Take stock of your voice and how you express yourself. A good negotiator uses a nice, low-keyed, pleasant voice to his best advantage. Speak slowly, clearly, whether you are on the telephone or sitting across a table. Your voice is an important tool; keep it working for you, not against you.

Remember, try to have a kindness in your voice. It's something people will respond to. I know I have felt better when talking to someone with a sympathetic way of speaking.

If you're a shouter, restrain yourself. If you're sarcastic by nature, try not to let it color your tone. If you have a bad attitude, it will come out in your voice as well as in the content of your conversation. So be careful of how your voice sounds to others. Keep in mind that the less threatening you sound, the more your adversary is going to feel comfortable with you. Think of your voice as part of your negotiating bedside manner. Be soothing. The "patient" will appreciate it.

Eye Contact

When you speak to someone, don't you want them to look you in the eye? If you don't, the message conveyed is that you are distracted, that what the other person is saying isn't all that important to you and you'd really rather not be there.

Don't underestimate the value of eye contact. When people talk to you in a negotiation, they want to persuade you. They have a profound need that you pay attention to them. It's a very important negotiating tool which helps you to convey interest and puts people at ease.

Most importantly, the impression created by not maintaining eye contact is of someone who cannot be trusted. You've heard people say adamantly, "Look me in the eye and say that!" Looking in someone's eyes when you are talking with them has become known as a measure of trustworthiness, as a test of your sincerity. Eye contact puts people at ease. It makes them comfortable. Al Testaverde said the reason I was retained was because I looked him straight in the eye.

No one makes eye contact better than Johnny Carson. Each night, he "negotiates" his guests through interviews. His goal isn't a contract, but simply good conversation. Appearing on "The Tonight Show" is an exciting but also nerve-wracking prospect. You feel as if you have to be an entertainer. When you arrive at the studio, unlike most other shows, you are given your own dressing room with your name on the door. Someone presses your clothes, brings you food and drinks, and caters to your every need. Then you sit in the green room, watching the guest before you. The pressure builds. You're waiting to get on and you know millions of people are going to be watching.

The next thing you know, the talent coordinator is smiling and saying, "You're on, Mr. Woolf." They accompany you right down the hall and to the place behind the curtain where you make your entrance. You're standing there, listening to Johnny Carson introduce you, and your heart is pounding. The last thing I thought of was my wife and kids, and I said to myself, "Here I go." It was the kind of feeling you must get before making a first parachute jump.

You step out and suddenly, there you are, sitting next to the most famous face on television. The point is that Carson knows how nervous his guests are, even if that guest is a big star. What separates Carson from anybody I have ever dealt with on television, and one of the things that makes him a great interviewer, is the simple fact that he gives you constant eye contact.

You are out there talking to him, still nervous, still unsure of yourself, when all of a sudden it seems like just the two of you having a friendly conversation. There may be twenty million people watching at home and a big audience just behind the cameras, but you don't even think of that. All you know is you're talking to Johnny Carson. He is looking directly at you, allowing you to shut out all the distractions and feel totally comfortable in what otherwise would remain a terrifying situation. Even during a break, he does all he can to put you at ease. During one commercial, he leaned over to me and joked that "alimony is the bounty *after* the mutiny" and "alimony is for services unrendered."

Why do I appreciate Johnny's approach so much? Because I have appeared on the program when he was not the host and the mood was definitely not the same. During those appearances, the guest host had written questions to ask me. He already knew what the answers would be. Eye contact wasn't maintained; we weren't having a conversation, just trading unrehearsed lines. This prevented any extensive eye contact and left us both feeling awkward and strange throughout the interview.

Perhaps the greatest antithesis to Carson's personable eye contact is Ted Koppel's late-night news program, "Nightline," where not only do guests not see Koppel, they don't see anyone. As a guest on that program, you sit in a studio and look into a camera with an audio plug in your ear. You don't dare take your eyes off the camera because you don't want to be scratching your nose or looking up in the air when Koppel asks you a question. Ted can see you, but you can't see him, which puts you at a great disadvantage when you are trying to communicate your thoughts to others. The experience made me that much more aware of the vital role eye contact fills in any dealings with people. As with so many other things, it's something you don't appreciate until you don't have it.

So, remember, when you're negotiating, use eye contact to put the other side at ease and reduce his anxiety. You'll not only make your negotiating partner happy, you'll make him more amenable to making an agreement.

Be a Good Listener

Listening well is a step beyond eye contact. The best way to learn a person's positions, problems, traits, likes, and dislikes is to listen intently. God gave us two ears and one mouth, so he must have intended that we listen twice as much as we talk.

Cable News Network talk show host Larry King, who is a friend and client, has a slew of anecdotes that illustrate the importance of listening well. He told me this story:

"I was a guest once on a morning show in Dallas. The woman who interviewed me was the classic hostess who asks you a question and then looks off in another direction, not paying any attention to your reply. She had five questions written out by someone else and she checked each one as she asked it. I noticed she wasn't listening at all. She was looking at the camera—anywhere but at me.

"Her third question was, 'What do you think is the secret to being a successful talk show host?'

"As I started to answer, I saw she was looking at the monitor, not paying me the slightest bit of attention. So I said, 'In my case, it's the fact that I'm an agent for the CIA. They get me good guests and I in turn say signal words for them every night for their agents.'

"Without missing a beat, she fired off her next question. 'Can you tell us some of the outstanding guests you've had?' Meanwhile, her whole crew was breaking up in the studio."

The inspiration for Larry's put-on was a classic bad interviewer routine by the comedy team of Bob and Ray, featuring their character, Wally Ballou. Wally would be on the street, saying, "This is Wally Ballou, world-famous interviewer. Here comes a gentleman. What is your name, sir?"

"My name is Jim Frizzell."

"Hello, Jim. Where do you live?"

"Long Island."

"What do you do for a living?"

"I'm an agent for the KGB."
"What brings you to New York?"
"I'm going to blow up the U.N. building."
"Have you seen *My Fair Lady*?"

Silence May Be Golden

You don't have to dominate a conversation to be successful. Silence can sometimes be a weapon. There may be times when you'll want to let the person on the other side just keep talking. *Let him talk.* He may reveal some information you may not have gotten if you had interrupted. As the saying goes, "The less said, the more heard."

Use silence as a strategy to plan your next move, not just as a timeout between your soliloquies. It is simply impossible to act sincerely interested in what somebody is saying or offering if you monopolize the conversation. Let your own silence speak for you occasionally.

There are other key reasons for intermittent silence. One, it may keep you from spouting off and saying the wrong thing. Sometimes the most important things are what you don't say. Two, by being silent, you might create the impression that you are agreeing with your opponent. That can create a little leverage for you as well as put the other side at ease. And it can afford you the opportunity to find out what he really wants.

Three, by being silent, you're not committing yourself to any position, and you show yourself to be deliberate, not rash. Four, silence gives the other side their day in court without being interrupted, something they are sure to appreciate.

Dressing for Respect

There is no second chance to make a first impression; make the first one count—in your favor. There is nothing new about this. You can't dress like a misfit and expect to be treated with respect. I am utterly astounded at the outfits some job applicants have worn into my office. If you are going to err, better to err on the side of formality. In any negotiation, you should dress better than you think you have to, even if you think an encounter will be fairly casual. Of course, if you're invited to play golf or tennis, or watch a football game with someone you're negotiating with, you should dress to fit the occasion or activity. A rule of thumb would be, take a look at yourself in a full-length mirror and ask yourself, "Would I like to do business with this person?" If not, go back and change!

What is appropriate and comfortable in California or Florida in the summer won't suit New England in the winter. Former NBC–TV President Grant Tinker would always be seen in New York in conservative attire; out in Hollywood, where an equal amount of business had to be done, he dressed casually, about one step above tennis togs.

A CBS executive once told me that when Dan Rather traveled into the Deep South to cover the civil rights movement in the 1960s, he always wore a suit—"my serious suit" he called it. The idea was to show he was there on serious business.

Dress in a dignified manner; no heavy gold chains with a half-opened shirt. No jeans and wrinkled T-shirts. Women don't need to dress exactly like their male counterparts. A woman's dress should convey the same kind of professionalism as does a man's traditional business suit.

Handling Your Ego

Before going into a negotiation, remember that parading your ego doesn't work. There's nothing wrong with a healthy ego, it gives you confidence and self-esteem. That's the side of the ego you have to show, but in a low-key way. I've faced enough ego-driven people to know that I've never been impressed or swayed by their self-aggrandizing displays. If your ego impels you to tell the other party how great you are and what your accomplishments are, ad nauseam, you will make an overbearing impression.

If you tell someone, "What do you mean you won't do it my way, don't you know who I am?" you won't be earning too many congeniality awards. My first reaction to someone like that is "What kind of a person am I dealing with?" Ignore this egotistical behavior and guide the talks back to the important issues. Displays of ego just get in the way of doing work.

Remember what Quincy Jones, who produced the song "We Are The World," said to Michael Jackson, Bruce Springsteen, Bob Dylan and the dozens of mega-stars before they worked through the night on the song? Jones advised them, "Check your egos at the door." If only negotiators would keep that thought in mind when getting together to do business.

Respect Everybody's Self-image

Not only do you need a good self-image to be an effective negotiator, you have to keep in mind that everybody has their own image of themselves. You would do well to try to determine—and respect— how other people think of themselves. If you mock someone's self-image, a good negotiation is at risk. A negotiation is almost like a marriage; if you show consistent disrespect for your spouse, the union won't survive.

No matter how wild or outlandish the lifestyle a person chooses, his self-image is vital to him. And if you don't honor a person's desire to respect his self-image, he'll know it. That goes for both someone you're negotiating with and someone you're negotiating for.

Take the case of Derek Sanderson, the flamboyant hockey player of the 1970s. At that time, Derek was on every major radio or TV show and had his picture on the cover of many major magazines. I once witnessed him giving six different interviews with six different reporters and then a day later denying everything he'd said to them. But even Derek, who didn't care what anybody said or wrote about him, called me one day from Toronto in a state close to apoplexy.

"Dammit, Bob," he shouted through the phone, "we'll get those sonsabitches. We'll get them."

"Take it easy," I said. "Calm down. What's this all about?"

He forced himself to lower his volume. "You know me," he said. "I usually don't mind what the guys write about me. They can write anything they want and I don't beef. But this story I can't believe. I'm looking at it with my own eyes and I still can't believe it! But here it is right in the paper. Right in the Toronto paper!"

I asked him to read the offending passage to me.

" 'Missing from the Bruins lineup last night,' " he said, " 'were superstar Bobby Orr, workhorse Johnny Bucyk and asshole Derek Sanderson.' "

So help me, that was how the sentence appeared in print. To this day, I have no idea how it happened, but I suspect some hockey fan in the composing room thought he would have a little fun, expecting someone down the line to catch his "humor." Somehow, no one did. It just slipped into print.

But there was no point in trying to explain that to Derek. Besides, I found the whole thing fairly amusing. I was laughing myself.

"This isn't funny," said Derek. "You know that, Bob. This isn't funny at all."

Wiping tears of laughter from my eyes, I tried to agree with him. "I understand, Derek. This is no laughing matter."

"I can take anything, Bob," he continued, "but not this. I'm going to sue. And before I'm finished, I'm going to own that paper and run that bastard out of town."

Trying to regain my poise, but not working awfully hard at it, I said, "I don't think we can do it."

"Why not?" he said, fuming. "We'll get that son of a bitch for libel. He can't do that to me."

"Well," I said, seriously, "in my professional opinion, we could never win the case. All they would have to do is go out and get your best friends for character witnesses, and they'd have to admit it was true. The truth is the best defense against libel."

I don't believe Derek appreciated my legal opinion—or my sense of humor. Of course, I loved Derek and was very close to him, so I felt I could tease him and get away with it.

I'm happy to report that the once wild and outrageous Derek is now a successful TV broadcaster and a highly respected staff member of the Mayor of Boston's Commission Against Drug and Alcohol Abuse, utilizing his endless charisma and past experiences to advise youngsters against the abuse of alcohol and drugs.

Everyone, no matter how flamboyant or outrageous, is conscious of his own dignity and self-image. Everyone has limits, and that's the moral here: if you don't respect a person's self-image, you violate his most valuable possession.

Be Extra Considerate

Common sense will tell you that it's poor judgment to say or do things that turn people off or disgust them. If it's not appropriate, don't smoke, drink, chew gum, or crack your knuckles. These are normal courtesies one follows in most interactions. Many times, being extra considerate can help keep the spirit of mutual agreement going even if your negotiations aren't moving all that well at that particular time.

When I was negotiating a contract for Gerald Wilkins with the New York Knicks, I was paired with the general manager of the basketball team, Al Bianchi. Gerald is the young, exciting guard whose brother, Dominique, is the Atlanta Hawks' spectacular forward. Gerald was improving every year and was a vital part of the Knicks' resurgence in 1988 and 1989.

Al and I met for several hours, but we were still far apart on terms for Gerald's new contract. We were both tired and a little discouraged as the meeting came to a close. However, a small extra gesture of politeness on Al's part breathed new life into my attitude. Al took the trouble to leave his office and walk me a considerable distance to the elevator doors down the hall from his office in Madison Square Garden. I felt that he was trying to let me know that even though we hadn't made much progress that day, he did want to come to an agreement. By extending that small courtesy, he was saying, *let's keep working at it*. His extra gesture eased my apprehensions about his determination to make a deal. We did eventually come to terms on an excellent contract for Gerald, which was achieved through extra efforts, both large and small.

Be Self-effacing

The first rules in real estate are location, location, and location. In the human relations game of negotiation, the rules are personalize, personalize, and personalize. Try to humanize yourself as much as possible. I frequently say something self-effacing like, "I'm the kind of guy who goes through half my life pulling on doors that say push." A sense of proportion and a little humor can show that you don't take yourself all that seriously, that you're a regular person. Again, it puts people at ease.

Remember Peter Falk's "Columbo" character on TV? This detective with the perpetually rumpled raincoat disguised a sharp deductive intellect with a manner that made him look like the last guy a police department would send out to solve a difficult crime. He'd ask seemingly innocuous and ridiculous questions that helped his investigation. The way Columbo played himself down made others feel a little superior, causing them to greatly underestimate him. He was most effective.

122

Don't Lose Your Composure

There will be times when you'll feel like exploding. You will feel indignant. You will feel taken advantage of. Take a deep breath and then forget it. You won't win by losing your composure. I am by nature a mild, even-tempered person, always trying to make things right and steer clear of an argument. I almost always rein in my anger. The few times I have lost my temper, I have always been the loser and regretted my lack of control.

I remember my experience with an all-American college football guard at the University of Alabama, who had been chosen as the fourth pick in the draft by the New England Patriots. I had just arrived at my winter home in Florida to spend a few days with my family when the prospect called from Boston and asked if we could meet. I cautioned him not to involve himself in any discussions with the Patriots. Almost any pleasantry an athlete expresses at that point, in a social or private setting, management will interpret as an anxiousness to sign. And they will use that as leverage. He promised me that he wouldn't do anything.

When we met the next morning, I learned that the young man had already visited the team's office and had discussed terms—exactly what I'd told him not to do! Having dropped everything to fly to Boston, I was more than mildly annoyed. I asked why he hadn't been honest with me in our conversation the night before. "I was afraid you wouldn't represent me," he said.

I told him he was right. I had made a special trip to help him. And now I lost my composure. "I can't deal with anyone who has lied to me," I said, and we ended our conversation.

Later that night, I calmed down and reviewed the situation dispassionately. Yes, he had been rude and perhaps he had misunderstood our plans. He was just a college senior and eager to start his pro career. Maybe I'd been a little harsh with him about his willingness to take matters into his own hands.

I called him the next morning to say that I had probably acted too

hastily and would be willing to meet again. He advised me that he had
signed with another representative. The player was John Hannah, whose
career lasted fourteen great years with the Patriots. He would be hailed
by *Sports Illustrated* and *The New York Times* as "the best guard ever to
play the game." Living in Boston, I had a lot of seasons to watch Hannah
grow in talent and maturity. I also spent many years regretting my
impatience and hasty judgment. I learned a lesson not only in dollars,
but by losing that special reward that comes from being involved with
someone who is among the best ever at what he does.

Office Style

When you call a new or old business associate, you want to be treated
with a certain level of respect. You expect the telephone to be answered
promptly, to be put on hold for a minimal time and to have a message
taken accurately. When you visit someone's office, you expect to be
asked promptly who you are, who you've come to see and to be able to
start your business apace.

If you negotiate as part of your in-office business, then your office staff must be efficient and polite, for the people who work for you
are an extension of you and your style as much as your manner, reputation, and clothes. They act and speak on your behalf and if their
manner is a turn-off to callers and visitors, it reflects badly on you
and affects you more than it affects your staff. That could mean lost
business.

I know one office where the receptionist lets the phones ring ten or
fifteen times because she's engrossed in the audio portion of a soap
opera. Or she's busy applying her makeup. Her phone messages often
convey little of what the caller said. On one message slip she had me
down as "Mr. Doof." So the person returned my call opening with, "Hi,
is Mr. Doof there?"

Once I called another attorney and asked a secretary if he was available. "No," she said, "he isn't. He's on the toilet." I didn't really want or need that little piece of information.

Here are some office rules I live by that actually enhance the style side of my negotiations:

1. Your staff should be aware of the people you do business with regularly or with whom you are negotiating. If the operator or secretary doesn't know someone is crucial to you, then important opportunities can be missed. I don't want the person at the other end of the line to be asked, "Does Mr. Woolf know who you are?" or "How do you spell your name, Mr. Sinatra?" If the phone is answered properly, you aren't giving your caller any reason to be disgruntled and you'll start your conversation on a pleasant note.

2. Read all letters that go out under your name. Make sure they are done professionally and the words are spelled correctly. Your clients and your adversaries judge you this way and view your correspondence as part of your style, care, and preparation. Sloppiness in a business letter may imply slovenly dealmaking.

3. Train your staff to remember names important to your business and to remember the names of support staff at other companies. Always treat support staff with respect. Not only is this the courteous way to treat people, in addition, someone you know one year as a mid-level executive may in five years be the company's CEO.

The Name Game

Remembering names is not one of my strengths. In fact, I wish everyone in the world wore name tags with big block letters like they do at conventions. A person's name is the most important thing in his life. It goes to the core of his dignity. Not remembering someone's name is really an insult to him. People try to get by with, "I recognize your face, but I can't recall your name." Although someone once said to me, "I remember your name, but I can't place your face."

It's always difficult for me when people come up to me and say, "Do you know me?" It can be embarrassing for both of us. Don't do it; it's only an ego trip for the person asking the question and can lead to hurt pride if the answer is "no."

If there is the slightest doubt that someone won't remember my name, I always give the other person my name first. I know Thomas P. "Tip" O'Neill, the former Speaker of the U.S. House of Representatives, very well and have been a guest at his home. But during a public occasion, where I realize I'm just one in a sea of faces greeting him and he could go blank seeing so many people, I repeat my name. It gives Tip, or anyone else in this potentially confusing milieu, a chance to say, "Why, of course, Bob, good to see you again."

There is a trick or two I have learned to try to overcome the predicaments of not remembering a person or his name. One, I always say, "It's nice to see you," rather than "Nice to meet you." I might have already met that person and what greater insult than to not remember meeting him. Two, when I am accompanied by another person and I run into someone whose name I have forgotten, I immediately introduce my friend, saying, "Say hello to Dr. Richard Greene," hoping that Mr. Nameless will respond with, "Hi, Dr. Greene, I'm Murray Munchkin."

If the world would adopt my mandatory name-tag plan, what happened to me one night would have been avoided. I was invited to a reception in honor of Rupert Murdoch, who had just acquired *The Boston Herald*. The Australian-born press lord had added another property to his American empire.

As I mingled with other guests, a reporter for a local TV station asked if he could film a brief interview with me. I was flattered to be singled out among the celebrities in attendance. Then the questions came: What did I think of the affair and the crowd? What changes did I plan to make at the paper?

126

By the second question, I knew we had a problem in identification. The reporter obviously thought I was Murdoch, a mistake that wasn't totally off-base, as we share a slight resemblance. But the interview was live and I met the challenges.

"First," I said, "I think all the employees at the *Herald* are grossly underpaid and I intend to review all the contracts and increase all the benefits."

The startled reporter managed to blurt out one word: "Really?"

Then I started laughing and said, "I think you have the wrong person." I have no idea if my interview aided Mr. Murdoch on his labor relations, but for fifteen seconds I had some wildly happy employees. I believe this reporter would vote in favor of my name-tag system.

In February 1985, shaking
hands with Donald Trump on
the day he made Doug Flutie
the highest-paid player in
professional football.
Courtesy of Richard Flutie

Playing catch on the
campaign trail with Michael
Dukakis at Des Moines,
Iowa, stopover. Michael is
much more regular than
people realize. *Courtesy of
John Dukakis*

With Dexter Manley at a news conference, as Dexter
makes his "manly" statement. *Courtesy of* The
Washington Post

Laughing all the way to the bank. From left to right, the Celtics' Sam Jones, Olympic High Jumper John Thomas, myself, Jon Morris of the Patriots, and the Celtics' John Havlicek. Though salaries in 1966 weren't that high to laugh about. *Courtesy of* The Boston Globe

Discussing strategy on upcoming contract negotiations with client and next-door neighbor, Larry Bird. *Courtesy of Ken Regan,* Time *magazine*

In Ted Turner's colorful office with Larry King and Ted after reaching an agreement on a contract with CNN. *Courtesy of Ted Turner*

My wife, Anne, and I at the White House with Carl Yastrzemski, who was receiving congratulations from President Jimmy Carter in 1979 on Yaz's 3,000 hits and 400 home runs. *Courtesy of The White House*

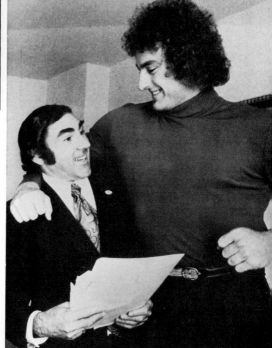

John Matuszak, the NFL's top draft choice in Toronto. This wire service photo on June 22, 1973, prompted fast action from the Oilers' Sid Gillman. *Courtesy of Associated Press*

On April 22, 1969, the Hawk unretires. Standing from left to right are Gabe Paul, then Cleveland president; Ken Harrelson next to me; American League president, Joe Cronin; and Dick O'Connell, Boston vice president. Seated is commissioner, Bowie Kuhn. *Courtesy of United Press International*

On August 1, 1972, Derek Sanderson signed his $2.65 million contract to become the highest-paid athlete in the world. *Courtesy United Press International*

Family portrait in 1971 with Anne, Gary, Stacey, Jim Plunkett, Randy Vataha, and long-time friend Ginny Campbell. Jim and Randy were like part of our family.

June 1989—dining out after Tiffany's high school graduation. From left to right are Anne, Gary, Stacey, me, and Tiffany.

With NBC "Today Show" star Gene Shalit. Gene is the one with the moustache.

Some lineup—George Bell 7'8"; Danny Schayes 7'; Kelly Tripucka 6'6"; me and my son Gary 5'10".

Appearing on the Johnny Carson show can be nerve-wracking, but his eye contact puts you at ease.

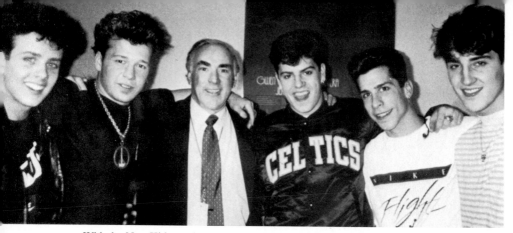

With the New Kids on the Block after their sold-out concert at the L.A. Forum. From left to right, Joe McIntyre, Donnie Wahlberg, me, Jordan Knight, Danny Wood, and Jonathan Knight. Jordan showed great courage wearing his Celtics jacket.

Heisman Trophy winner Vinny Testaverde in my office awaiting 1987 draft. He was the number one pick in the country.

At the home of Anwar Sadat in Cairo, Egypt, with his daughter Camelia and his first wife, Ekbal.

Staying in shape for when it was going to happen big, including Peter Work, tour manager. Foreground: New Kids on the Block's road manager, Peter Work, and me. Surrounding us, the New Kids: Danny Wood, Joe McIntyre, Donnie Wahlberg, Jordan Knight, and Jonathan Knight. *Courtesy of Peter Work*

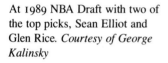

All happy in 1969 when John Havlicek decided to stay in Boston. Red Auerbach is seated.

At 1989 NBA Draft with two of the top picks, Sean Elliot and Glen Rice. *Courtesy of George Kalinsky*

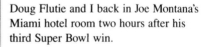

Doug Flutie and I back in Joe Montana's Miami hotel room two hours after his third Super Bowl win.

While in Jerusalem with an all-star touring team. How often do you see a picture of Larry Bird on a camel?

Anne and I visiting Japan with Joe and Jennifer Montana for Pearl Bowl IV (Japanese version of the Super Bowl) at Tokyo Dome, during the summer of 1989.

Meeting with potential client while at Tokyo Dome—he said he was a wide receiver. I agreed.

Visiting with Prince Charles, Princess Diana, and Armand Hammer at the royals' summer home at Highgrove. Note Anne shaking hands with Princess Diana. *Courtesy of Armand Hammer*

CHAPTER SIX

Leverage

"It is circumstances and proper timing that give an action its character
and make it either good or bad."

> —AGESILAUS II (444–360 B.C.), former King of
> Sparta

"You can get much farther with a kind word and a gun, than you can
with a kind word alone."

> —AL CAPONE, infamous user of leverage

NOW THAT we've gathered all of our information and know how we are
going to use it, the time has come to assess our leverage. Leverage is the
strength of each party's position and it is the key strategic element in any
negotiation. When I look at the leverage in a negotiation I ask, who has
it and who doesn't? Who has the better bargaining position and why?
How can I use my leverage to my greatest benefit?

As I keep analyzing, every reason that the other side wants or needs an agreement is my leverage—provided that I know those reasons, and every reason that I want or need an agreement is the other side's leverage—provided they know those reasons.

A knowledge of as many reasons the other side may have for needing the agreement is to my advantage. Hopefully, my preparation has given me this knowledge. Conversely, I try not to give any information to the other side that would provide leverage for them.

When each side's position is known, you make your first assessment of strengths and weaknesses. As talks progress, events, positions, and attitudes change, so you must assess leverage over and over again.

When you utilize leverage, you are doing all you can to maximize your strong points and minimize your weaknesses, while doing the reverse with your opponent's case. Always keep in mind your opponent is also doing this. It's like a chess game. Each move changes the position of the board; the right moves at the right time can endanger your opponent's king. So you must always assess how and when to use your leverage to the most advantage.

You *must* be constantly aware of changes in leverage. If you aren't, you may lose yours. If you need emergency surgery, the surgeon has all the leverage. You're not going to quibble over his fee while you're rolling on a gurney to the operating room. But if you want to buy a company whose stock price has just taken a tumble, your leverage increases because the other side is dramatically weaker.

It's not entirely the analysis of powerful positions that creates leverage. It's how that power is applied. You can use it subtly or with a hammer. You can apply it when conditions are right and when you look your best, or use it at the wrong time and ruin your advantage.

Analyzing leverage is a subtle game. You can determine a lot from the actual facts of a situation, but perceptions also play a part. Again, your opponent will do the same thing. Wars are sometimes won not by the armies you have, but the armies they *think* you have. Remember, the Japanese surrendered to us in World War II, thinking we had a huge arsenal of atomic bombs. We had detonated the only two bombs we had on Hiroshima and Nagasaki, but Japan did not know this vital information and so they surrendered and the war was ended. They thought we had all the leverage when in fact we didn't have any.

You'll be assessing how much the other side wants or needs what you have, and how much you want or need what the other side has. Who *needs* it more? Who has the greater motivation? If you determine the other side's needs are greater than its wants, you have the advantage.

Go Gently into Those Good Talks

I think it's clear by now that I like to approach a negotiation in a fair and calm way. How you use leverage can be one of the touchiest moments in reaching an agreement. In my own mind, when I've got more leverage, I'm going to capitalize on it. But I don't act that way. When I'm certain that my bargaining partner has to meet the price I'm asking, I'll say something like, "I'm sorry, but that's really what my client needs and I don't think we can go down," not, "You've got nowhere to go on this. Sign my client or you'll lose your right fielder forever." There's no sense in gloating over the leverage you may have over an opponent because while you might have the leverage now, your opponent may have it the next time.

It's rare when you have full leverage. You can hope and pray for it. You will rarely be in the catbird seat like the plumber you call when your pipes have burst and your basement is flooded with a foot of water. The plumber has all the leverage. After all, what are you going to do, slosh around in the water and *bargain*?

Take Note

I always write down as much as possible about every negotiation I'm involved in. So before a negotiation starts, I'll make a checklist of everything I can, including the leverage I have and the leverage I think my opponent has. I'll keep that list before me throughout the negotiation, and make notes as the talks progress. I want to keep aware of every possible change and nuance of the negotiation that can alter either side's leverage. There's nothing more embarrassing for me than to miss something my opponent says that can affect my leverage. The notes are especially helpful when talks extend beyond one meeting. You can't remember everything, so you want to be able to refer to what has happened in previous meetings.

I Had All the Leverage, but It Turned into the 100 Days' War

The year before Larry Bird arrived in Boston, the Celtics had a dreadful season of only twenty wins and sixty-two losses. They needed Larry desperately and Red Auerbach, the Celtics' president, knew it. Wins were scarce and attendance at Boston Garden was sparse. That's why Red had made Larry his number one draft choice in 1978, a full year before Larry graduated from Indiana State. Red was willing to wait a year to get what he wanted, a shrewd but risky move that characterized Red's successful style.

I knew Red would stomp and scream when it came to negotiating Larry's first pro contract, but I thought the Celtics' deep need for a savior to rescue the team from the worst doldrums in its history would be all the leverage I needed to quickly reach a lucrative deal on Larry's behalf. Was I wrong! Instead, I got a war run by General Auerbach.

Red is easily the most intimidating person I know. He thinks the offer he puts on the table is the best one he can make. And he stands by it, and tries to frighten his opponent into agreeing with him. That's negotiating the Auerbach way. When I make speeches, I tell this story about Red:

When Red was a little boy, he wrote a letter to God. He said, "Dear

God, if you send me down a train set, I'll be good for two weeks."
Sensing he had ceded the Almighty too much, he said, "Naahh," and
ripped up the letter.

"Dear God," Red began his second letter, "if you send me a train
set, I'll be good for one week." He thought about it and ripped up the
letter. Just then his mother came into his room and said, "Red, I'm going
to take you to church so you can see how other people worship."

While Red was at the church, he saw a statue of the Virgin Mary
and he decided to take it home with him. Then he wrote God again,
saying, "Dear God, if you ever want to see your mother again . . ."

That was Red. He was also the man who built the greatest dynasty
in sports. But even he knew the Celtics had fallen on hard times. The
team was drawing few fans to their games. The city of Boston was
anxiously awaiting Larry's arrival. For more than a year, die-hard fans
anticipated Bird. Larry's senior year at Indiana State was covered by
Boston newspapers as if he were playing at Boston College. He was a star
in Boston and yet there was no certainty he would ever set foot on the
parquet floor of Boston Garden. So you can imagine who would be
faulted if Larry didn't sign with the Celtics: Red Auerbach, right?
Wrong. Me.

Two days after I was chosen to represent Larry, I brought him to
Boston. Larry made a dramatic first appearance at Boston Garden on
April 6, 1979, arriving with Auerbach, Celtics owner Harry Mangurian,
and me during halftime of a game against the Denver Nuggets. Larry got
a standing ovation from the small crowd. But two days later, as Larry and
I visited the Celtics' locker room after a game against the New Jersey
Nets, Red and I had a disagreement. Red tried to tell Larry what to do,
saying all kinds of things that indicated that the master manipulator was
trying to control Larry.

I had previously arranged with Larry that if Red tried to intimidate
us, we would establish that Red couldn't get away with it. So in front of
Red, I called Larry aside.

"Larry," I said, "who represents you?"

"You do, Mr. Woolf," he said.

"Larry," I said, "if I tell Red we're not going to sign with Boston, what's going to happen?"

"We're not going to sign with Boston," Larry replied.

"If I tell you we're going to sign with the Celtics, what's going to happen?" I said.

"We'll sign with the Celtics," he said.

I turned to Red. "Did you hear that, Red? Is there any doubt in your mind what's going to happen?"

Red hollered and screamed and I just turned and left the room. I told a reporter, "Auerbach is already trying to intimidate me."

I went directly to Mangurian. "Red and I don't seem to be communicating very well," I said, "and I'm afraid the result will be that you're not going to be able to sign Bird." Well, Harry blew up. He was so angry that he was out of control, so unlike his usual public image as a paternal, generous man.

The next day, the Woolf-Auerbach "battle" was the top of the sports news and I was being painted the villain. A few days later, Auerbach came to my office and we tried to start negotiating on more amicable footing. I had a list of requests drawn up by the Terre Haute committee that had chosen me to represent Larry. They said to me, "Would you mind asking for a $1 million per year salary, an apartment, and a car?" I knew Red would reject them all, but I figured it wouldn't hurt to ask. In one of those rare instances, it did hurt.

I said to Red, "I have to ask you a bunch of things that may be a little unreasonable, but I gave my word that I would ask them." So I asked, and as I expected, Red said no to all of them. With that out of the way, I then suggested to Red that I felt the opening offer had to be at least $500,000. He offered me the $500,000 and I said, "Okay, we'll meet again soon."

The next day the war started. Red tricked me. All over the *Boston Globe* and *Boston Herald-American* blared headlines highlighting the Committee's requests that both Red and I knew were merely opening gambits. Now I was the enemy: "Woolf Wants Six Years for $6 Million!" "Woolf Wants Apartment!" "Woolf Wants Car!" The writers took off after me, saying I was greedy, that I was trying to hold up the Celtics, that after waiting a year and a half for their salvation, I was depriving the city of Larry Bird!

Thus began what the Boston press called "The Hundred Days' War." I received obscene phone calls. My kids were insulted at school. A cartoon in the *Boston Globe* depicted me as a bandit holding up the Celtics.

It really got ridiculous. At one point during our battle, a friend's son met Red at a bar mitzvah and walked over to greet him.

"I'm a friend of your nephew's," said the young man.

"Isn't that nice," said Red cordially.

"I'm also a friend of Gary Woolf's," he added.

Hearing my son's name, Red replied, "Big deal."

People who would normally be kind to me became angry. I was coming home from a speaking engagement in Worcester and I was stopped at a red light. I asked the man driving the car next to me how to get back to Boston.

"You're Bob Woolf," said the man. "When are you going to sign Larry Bird?"

"I don't know," I said.

"Then I don't know how to get to Boston," the man said, and drove off.

Despite the misery it was causing me, I knew what Red was doing. I didn't have to like it. This was his way of negotiating the biggest contract in Celtics history. He didn't have much leverage and he was doing everything he could to manufacture some by knocking me and accusing me of holding up the whole Bird-signing process. While I was being accused of asking for $1 million per year, the press was told Red would pay only $500,000 per year.

As a matter of fact, at several times, Red said to me, "How do you like the number I'm doing on you?" I could only say, "My compliments to the chef."

After negotiating many times, to no avail, Red called a press conference. "We've called off negotiations with Woolf," he said. "We're not going to negotiate anymore on Larry Bird. I gave them my best shot and they said, 'No way.' I may just sit back and wait for the draft. If I blow it, I blow it . . . I could eat [this contract]. If I do, he'll never get the contract I'm offering. I guarantee that. No one will pay him if he doesn't play." Over and over, I heard him say on television, "I will never pay Larry Bird more than $500,000."

Three weeks into the impasse, I called a press conference in Indiana. I said the next move was up to the Celtics, to move beyond their $500,000 offer. "If the Celtics wish to remain with their first and only offer," I said, "then as much as we'd like to be with Boston, we will choose to go elsewhere or enter the 1979 draft in June."

But the war dragged on through May and early June. I still felt I had the leverage to make a good deal, so I was going to stick to my guns. Red used every trick in the book. He accused me of negotiating with the Chicago Bulls, who would have a chance at Bird if the Celtics didn't sign him. He questioned the legitimacy of the Terre Haute committee, accusing it of violating the National Collegiate Athletic Association's rules by serving as a de facto agent before Larry was drafted. He was trying everything!

Now the Celtics had to do something, if only to save face for Red. He was not going to be the one to raise his offer. So owner Harry Mangurian became involved, and along with Red and Jan Volk, we were able to meet and reach an agreement to pay Larry $650,000 a year.

Red knew all along what he had done to me and once the contract was completed, he changed faces. The generous Red came to the press conference announcing Larry's signing. Before any questions were asked, Red told me, "Everything's fine with us. I'm going to make you look good now in the city and make sure everything's like it was before." Red then got up and told nearly 100 newspaper, radio, and TV reporters assembled in a private club room in Boston Garden, "I never really had any disagreement with Bob Woolf. Bob Woolf is always a gentleman." I almost fainted.

And sure enough, I quickly moved from angry fans cursing and gesturing at me obscenely with a certain finger, to joyous fans waggling another finger to indicate, "We're number one."

Larry and I got what we wanted. I moved Auerbach $150,000 per year above what he wanted to pay. And everyone ended up happy, knowing that Larry Bird was finally a Celtic.

There's Nothing Better than Competition

When you have nowhere else to turn, you're in trouble. When you have somewhere else to go, you are competitive. In a negotiation, a competitive offer pumps up talks, changes the market value of my client, and makes his employer think twice about telling him to leave. Whenever I bring a competitive offer to a negotiating table, the direction of the talks invariably changes.

You've seen it in action. You want to buy a house and the seller says, "You'll have to act quickly because somebody else has offered more than you did." Or in highly public sports negotiations where a baseball free agent has had as many as twelve teams vying for his services. One team's offer plays against the other and against the other and so on.

Competitive bidding puts pressure on who you negotiate against. It raises the possibility on the other side that you may end your talks with him, not because you don't like him or find him difficult to negotiate with, but because there's something better out there. If the first bidder truly needs what you have, he is likely to up his offer. That might introduce a price spiral that makes little sense logically. But remember, it only takes one buyer to set the market value.

This is how Derek Sanderson skated into a fortune. Even though he was purposely abrasive, exasperating and arrogant, Derek was a tremendously appealing hockey player for the Boston Bruins. Straight out of junior hockey, he signed a three-year contract paying him $10,000, $12,000, and $14,000 a year. Halfway through his contract, he told anyone who'd listen, "I'm getting paid peons' wages. I'm paid like a common laborer. I'd be better off picking fruit."

Derek had never scored thirty goals. He had yet to receive a single vote for the all-star team. But he had a captivating personality and was a fan favorite. His flamboyant personality kept him in the press almost daily. So when the time came to sign a new contract, it wasn't surprising that in addition to my own negotiations, Derek conducted his own in the press.

In retaliation, the Bruins held a press conference to air their side of the story, including how much salary and bonus money they had paid Sanderson over the years. During the 1970–71 season, he received $14,000 in salary plus a $10,000 bonus. Even though it's hard to believe now, at that time, this was a fair salary. That it was a fair contract was an irrelevant concept to Derek. He thought he was worth a lot more.

I had no leverage when I began negotiations. Derek's rights to play in the National Hockey League were held by the Boston Bruins, so he could either play for the Bruins or not play at all. We hassled and haggled down to the last minute. Finally, at two o'clock in the morning, we reached an agreement: $25,000 for one year. They had all the leverage.

Sometime in 1972, we heard rumors about a new league forming, the World Hockey Association. Our first contact was with a man named Herb Martin, who had rights to the Miami franchise. "What would it take," he asked during our first meeting, "to get Sanderson away from the Bruins and down to Miami?"

Finally, I had leverage. I had a bidder new to the game, with a talented, high-profile client they wanted badly. It was the WHA strategy for each team to wrest one star from each NHL team and use him as a marquee attraction. Derek fit the bill perfectly.

"In the first place, Herb," I said, "I don't think Derek will ever leave. He loves Boston and the Bruins. Despite what he says, he loves the team. But I'll tell you this much. He won't leave for anything less than $250,000 a year." The figure, ten times his salary, was a wild stab for me.

Martin didn't blink. "That sounds fair," he said. "We'll take care of that. But it will have to be long-term. Something like ten years."

That was $2.5 million for ten years, a totally unheard-of figure, coming two years before Catfish Hunter became baseball's highest-paid player at $2.8 million over five years. But when the time came to put up the money, Martin couldn't produce it. My leverage seemed to have disappeared, but it returned miraculously when the Philadelphia franchise, led by an attorney named Jim Cooper, came forward. Cooper was a hockey nut. He'd go anywhere to watch a game. He said to me, "What will it take to get Sanderson away from the Bruins. How can I do it?"

The leverage was all mine again and it put me in a new position. For years, I had cajoled team owners to come up with the money to pay my client. Now I was determining the amount needed to close a deal. I was establishing fair market value.

The options were mine: I could allow Derek to stay in Boston or sign him to Philadelphia where he could be the symbol of his new team and the new league. Derek was the most colorful and controversial player in hockey, and if we chose not to play, the WHA had little else to turn to, they could not have needed him more.

After thinking about Cooper's question, I replied, "Make him the highest paid athlete in the world. If you do that, Derek might bite. Otherwise, if it isn't anything sensational, he won't do it. The idea of making more money than any other player in sports would make him flip."

It never hurts to ask. The new league needed Sanderson more than Derek needed the WHA. Cooper bought the logic. Before the day was over, we had outlined a $2 million package. After several calls and one more face-to-face session, we worked out a multiyear, $2.65 million deal, which was happily signed by Derek.

The Bruins had the opportunity to sign Sanderson but had procrastinated. Indeed, the entire NHL misread both the participants involved and the leverage at play. The NHL owners underestimated the strength of the new league's willingness to act as a competitive bidder and lost many star players to the new league.

Nine Million Nuggets—and My Leverage Works Perfectly

When I negotiated a new contract for Danny Schayes, a seven-foot center for the Denver Nuggets, I found myself with plenty of leverage. Danny has a great basketball pedigree: his dad, Dolph, of the old

Syracuse Nationals, was one of the greatest players in the early days of pro basketball and a member of the Basketball Hall of Fame.

In the NBA, centers are kings. They are the building blocks of their teams and can command huge salaries. Patrick Ewing, Akeem Olajuwon and Moses Malone, three of the best centers in the league, earn between $1.9 million and $3 million a year. When it came time to negotiate a new contract for Danny, it was in the context of that shortage. Danny is a fine center, and the Nuggets had no replacement for him.

Danny earned $400,000 in the final year of his last contract. He was a totally free agent, so he could sign with another team and the Nuggets would get no compensation in return—my leverage. When the 1988 season ended, it was time to negotiate a new agreement with Nuggets' general manager, Pete Babcock.

His first offer was a three-year contract with annual salaries of $475,000, $500,000 and $525,000. The negotiations were fairly public, and the local papers were saying the team should sign Schayes—more leverage for me. Gradually, I was able to get the first year of the contract up to $800,000. Meanwhile Danny's telling me, "Okay, okay, I'll sign," and I'm saying, "Be patient."

Then Denver increased the bid to $1 million a year.

Up until now, I had not received any offers from other teams. But then I began to receive a few calls, the most seriously interested team was the Phoenix Suns and their general manager, Jerry Colangelo, made the call. He said he was very interested and after several conversations with him, he made an offer of $1.2 million per year for Danny.

Now, I was able to do more than make suggestions to the Nuggets. There was genuine competitive bidding and as far as I was concerned that immediately increased Danny's value: he now had another place to go to if Denver couldn't sign him. I explained to Colangelo that I would like to keep negotiating with him, but that I would also continue to negotiate with Denver and the other teams that had called.

I didn't think Denver would go any higher, but I felt it would have been unethical to have Danny sign elsewhere without at least giving

Denver a chance to bid. Now, I had three strong pieces of leverage working for me:

1. The Nuggets needed Schayes badly.
2. Public pressure was on Babcock to sign Schayes.
3. I had a competitive bidding situation.

The only real leverage the Nuggets had was unknown to them. Danny didn't really want to go anywhere else. He preferred to stay in Denver and told me so. He had taken away some of my power to negotiate harder with Denver, but only Danny and I knew that. All the Nuggets knew was that they lost on the court and in public if they did not sign Danny.

So I told Babcock, "Look, I have another offer that makes your offer seem out of line. It's a question of whether you want to live with these new figures." Since I felt I could get Phoenix up to $1.5 million a year with further negotiating, I told Babcock that the asking price for Schayes was now up to $1.5 million a year, given the other team's serious interest.

Now it's big-time poker. The Nuggets can say, "No, we won't pay that kind of money"—a form of dubious leverage, considering what they would lose by passing on Danny—but I felt they wouldn't. They had to have Schayes, and they had to face up to it.

"I can only do $1.2 million," said Babcock.

"That's most probably not going to be enough," I said. "But, let's keep working on it."

Even when you have the lion's share of the leverage, don't rub it in. So I waited. We didn't have a firm deadline, and I exhibited little urgency.

So, without the leverage that would enable the team to tell me to reduce my requests or tell me to walk away, the Nuggets signed Danny for close to $1.5 million a year for six years, fully guaranteed, and he was able to stay with the team he had wanted to be with all along. Nine million dollars because of leverage enhanced by competitive bidding. Both sides ended up happy.

A Hawk Threatens to Fly the Coop

When you have the leverage, you can win big. If you have something someone wants *badly*, you can control the bidding. In the case of Ken "Hawk" Harrelson, I had all the leverage, and *nobody* was able to diminish it.

It's hard to believe, but it was more than twenty years ago that Hawk Harrelson was flying high as the flamboyant, long-haired slugger for the Boston Red Sox. In 1968, he was the American League Player of the Year, hitting thirty-five homers and knocking in 109 runs. Almost out of nowhere, Hawk was the biggest event in baseball. Boston worshipped him. He lived as high as he could in a plush apartment, with a wardrobe of fifty suits, fifty pairs of shoes, and a houseboy who kept it all in order.

For a brief while, Harrelson was bigger than other Red Sox heroes like Carl Yastrzemski, Jim Lonborg, and Tony Conigliaro, whose tragic eye injury in 1967 eventually ended his promising career.

The Red Sox were so happy with Harrelson's performance that they ripped up his 1968 contract and raised him from $35,000 to $50,000 for 1969. He was a *very* hot property. But shockingly, just two weeks into the 1969 season, the Red Sox announced that they had traded Harrelson to the Cleveland Indians in a five-player swap.

When Hawk reached me in a hotel room in Arizona, he was apoplectic. "You're not going to believe this, Bobby," he wailed to me, "but they have just traded my rear end to Cleveland. Can you believe that baloney? Cleveland! Can you believe it?"

I couldn't. I told him to sit tight and not do anything or say anything, a mean feat for the unpredictable Hawk. But I didn't have any advice to give him. I was too shocked. I promised that I'd have a plan by my return to Boston the next morning.

My head was spinning, but I came up with an angle: we'll *retire* Hawk! It was risky. It was bold. But I believed we had the leverage. He was a star and a productive hitter who put people in the seats. While I knew he'd probably have to report to Cleveland, I sensed that it would be worth it to make Boston and Cleveland think he'd retire, which would undo the trade and benefit nobody.

When I returned home, I called a press conference in my office, which was crammed with reporters from Boston and around the country. Tearfully, the Hawk informed the press and the world, "This is the last time you'll ever see the Hawk in baseball. The Hawk's not going to do it anymore. I can't hardly believe it myself."

"What will you do for work, Hawk?" asked one of the many skeptical reporters.

"I'll work in my sub shops," the Hawk quipped.

Rather than having Hawk say arrogantly and abruptly, "I ain't leavin' Boston," we made it clear that it was "economically unfeasible" for him to go to Cleveland. We gave the impression that Hawk made more money from his off-the-field businesses in Boston than he did inside Fenway Park. So he could take baseball—or leave it. What baseball didn't know or bother to find out was that if Harrelson left Boston, his businesses would fall apart.

The story got huge national exposure, which added to our leverage. The national press was siding with Harrelson, even if the Boston reporters were on the management's side. But we had done something nobody else had ever done: we'd thrown everything back to the management, something that would have been crazy with a less-talented ballplayer.

But remember, this was in the time before free agency when ballplayers were free to leave their teams for the best offer. This was still the time of the reserve clause, where team owners owned players in perpetuity. Withholding services from a team was unprecedented in sports labor history. This would be a major test of how much baseball really needed Harrelson.

So let's sum up the leverage to this point:

1. Harrelson was a talented player whom neither Cleveland nor Boston could afford to be without.
2. He was a crowd draw who could put a lot of money into an owner's pocket.

3. The season had already begun, and a decision had to be made quickly. I believed the decision could only benefit the Hawk.
4. There were other players involved in the trade waiting to find out where they were going.

The press conference produced quick action. Boston general manager Dick O'Connell and Cleveland general manager Gabe Paul met us for a meeting at the "21" restaurant in Manhattan. We didn't get anywhere. We were just feeling each other out. But I knew that O'Connell and Paul were looking for a way to resolve the situation.

On the way back to Boston, I candidly told the Hawk, "I know all this really upsets you, but baseball is your game. You can't make the kind of living you want right now outside doing anything else. How much will it take to get you to go to Cleveland?"

"I don't know, Bob," he said, looking at me carefully. "The money is in your department. What do *you* think?"

"Six figures," I said instantly, "You would need six figures."

The answer pleased the Hawk immensely. "Oh, wow, the Hawk, a hundred-thousand-dollar ballplayer! How are we going to do it?"

"We're going to wait for them to make an offer," I said.

The Hawk and I were summoned the next day to New York for a meeting with baseball commissioner Bowie Kuhn, American League president Joe Cronin, Paul, and O'Connell.

After presenting our positions, Kuhn asked Hawk and me to wait in another room while they met privately. Thirty minutes later, O'Connell offered Harrelson a raise to $75,000 if he would sign a two-year contract.

I said no. In a few minutes, they returned with a new offer: $75,000 for the first year, $100,000 for the second.

I asked to speak alone to Hawk. He was pleading with me. "Take it, take it," he said. I said no. "It's five o'clock. They've got a whole hallway full of reporters out there and Bowie Kuhn is not going to let them spoil it for another lousy $25,000. If they've come this far, they'll go all the way."

So I said no again. They conferred once more. The Hawk was angry. He was convinced they wouldn't go all the way. "They're not going to do it," he said.

Twenty minutes later, the door opened. I had fallen asleep. I had not slept in days since Hawk's call to me in Arizona.

But O'Connell was ready with another offer. They agreed to forgive a $19,000 loan if he accepted the offer for $75,000 in the first year and $100,000 in the second. Adding $19,000 to $75,000 brought the figure to $94,000. Close enough, I was sold.

The leverage we had dictated the offers. I never asked for anything specific. I never made a threat. I let them come to me. The situation that I had created, whereby he would retire, had created leverage where there had been none.

When all was over, Commissioner Kuhn invited me to take a picture with Paul, O'Connell, Cronin, and himself. It was a dignified gesture and signaled to me that baseball was starting to grudgingly accept a player's attorney within their midst.

When You Have All the Leverage—Utilize It

There are times when you may find that you have all the leverage. Don't ever miss this opportunity to maximize the benefits of this position. In January of 1990, when Joe Montana led the San Francisco 49'ers to their fourth Super Bowl victory, he became the most sought-after athlete in America. In fact, I had to hire two full-time staff members just to handle the incoming calls and to answer the piles of mail that arrived at my office everyday. Joe was hot and everybody knew it, so it was a matter of negotiating the most advantageous contract terms for endorsements and commercials for Joe. I made sure that I took advantage of the overwhelming leverage and negotiated long-term, guaranteed contracts at the highest range of the fair market value for Joe's services.

* * *

Since leverage can often turn in your favor quickly, you need to be ready to gather information right away in order to utilize the change in events. When the recording group, the New Kids on the Block, signed their first recording contract, their leverage was no more than that of any other unproven act. They signed a standard entry-level type of agreement with a low percentage of profits being paid to them. However, when the Kids' first album went platinum, Columbia Records couldn't keep up with the volume of demand for their album. It soon became obvious to everyone in the music industry that a phenomenon similar to the meteoric rise of the Beatles was occurring with the New Kids on the Block. Given their huge and sudden success, the Kids' management team immediately began to research the contract terms of other "Super Groups" and approached Columbia Records in an effort to negotiate a new contract that would be more in line with the Kids' exceptional accomplishments. Columbia Records acknowledged that the original contract was now outmoded and unfair, and a much more beneficial contract was agreed upon.

You Can't Always Get What You Want

Don't always expect to get everything you want. You may have all the leverage. You may have very little. You may run into an unpredictable opponent. In the course of a negotiation, the leverage you hold for your client may plummet due to an injury, bad ratings, or a low stock price. Likewise, your leverage may soar due to events that increase the need for your client's product or service. Even when I feel I'm on a roll in a negotiation and I think my leverage will win out, I've occasionally underestimated the loyalty my client feels for his employer, sending my leverage sinking like Gaylord Perry's spitball.

I Thought I Had All the Leverage, But I Miscalculated on One Little Thing

By the fall of 1987, Larry King was one of the nation's most popular and well-known cable and radio personalities, with evening talk shows on Cable News Network and Mutual Radio. Now I planned to use the popularity Larry had as a cornerstone at CNN during contract negotiations with CNN's owner, the maverick capitalist Ted Turner. Turner inspires deep loyalty among his workers and nobody, it turned out, was more loyal to Ted than Larry King.

I figured I had almost all the marbles. Larry was at the zenith of his popularity. His nighttime talk show was hot, and Turner knew Larry's value had soared far beyond the value of his current salary. Based on his ratings and popularity, Larry was drastically underpaid. My leverage was that other, very powerful people in broadcasting knew that, too.

Huge seven-figure offers were flowing in. ABC News' Roone Arledge wanted Larry to follow Ted Koppel's "Nightline" every evening. Michael and Roger King of King World wanted to syndicate Larry as they had syndicated Oprah Winfrey, "Jeopardy!" and "Wheel of Fortune." Fox Television owner Rupert Murdoch wanted Larry as a building block for his fledgling independent network.

All three offered something CNN didn't: broadcast exposure. At the time, only half of the people with televisions could get cable. So in addition to more money, which could be had from either one, I had the added leverage that Larry would reach more viewers than he could at CNN. I thought Larry's relationship with Turner would be my ultimate leverage in getting what Larry really wanted, a new, long-term deal to stay at CNN. King and Turner are very close friends and I figured that Turner would do everything possible to keep Larry in the family.

So I flew down to CNN's Atlanta headquarters where I told Turner, "We'd like a substantial raise. We're getting this offer from Murdoch, this offer from King World, and this offer from Arledge, etc."

The competitive offers served only to make Ted take the role of the poor relation, not the rich uncle.

"I hear what you're saying," he said, "but I can't pay those sums of money. It would throw off my whole payroll. In fact, he makes more money than I do now. If there's any way I could do it, I would. You've got to believe me. If there's any way I could do it, I would. But there's no way to do it without destroying the whole organization."

"If you can't be competitive," I said, "unfortunately, then we would have to seriously consider our other offers."

Then Turner went wild. "Let me call Larry," he said. This is my nightmare—the persuasive Turner talking directly to the ultra-loyal King. So Ted calls Larry, who's in Los Angeles this day. It was only six in the morning.

"I love you, Larry," Turner said. "How could you leave me? You're like a brother to me. If I had a sandwich, I'd give you half. If I had fifty cents, I'd give you a quarter. Stay with me."

"Okay," Larry said, "I'll stay."

I was shocked. Just like that, my leverage was nearly spent. I could no longer use the other offers to raise Ted's. True, we eventually agreed on a salary that was a substantial raise for Larry, but still not as much as I wanted. However, I did negotiate a six months' notice clause for Larry's departure from CNN if he so decided during the term of the contract. I'll be ready next time.

When You Don't Have Leverage

You will not always have the leverage. In many cases you won't. That's not the time to give up and give in. You still have your wits and creativity about you and, if fairness prevails on the other side, you might get a little leverage even if you don't have any on paper. It won't happen all the time, but it does happen.

Call this the "Just Say Please" tactic.

Suppose that a hotel says it has no reservations. The hotel has 1,000 rooms, but not a space for the day you need it. That is indeed leverage; you want something they don't even have. You can say, "Please, I understand you have no rooms, but among 1,000 customers, somebody is bound to cancel out. Please put me on a waiting list and I'll even send you a check in advance to prove my faith in your finding a room for me." Don't be surprised if it works.

Or, if you are dissatisfied with a product or service, you can tell a storeowner or service person that if something isn't repaired, you will one, call a lawyer, two, bring in the local department of consumer affairs or Better Business Bureau, or three, inform his or her boss or a company president of a subordinate's mishandling of your problem.

I'm not saying these kinds of things always work, but they do create positive alternatives to the word "no."

I Had No Leverage, but I Sure Showed Them

When I'm lecturing at law schools, colleges, and universities, the question I'm always asked is, "After all your negotiations, what's the toughest you've ever had?"

It may come as a surprise to you, given my varied experiences, but my toughest negotiation was for a contract on behalf of . . . my local rabbi.

Sure, you don't expect rabbis to even have contracts. But some do. And a few years ago, the rabbi of my temple in Brookline asked me for my help in getting him a raise. I was intrigued and charmed. I could play good neighbor and practice my craft in my own neighborhood.

I met with the congregation. I met with the sisterhood. I met with the brotherhood. I got absolutely nowhere. They told me that attendance at the weekly services was down, that membership was down and donations were down. They couldn't justify granting the rabbi a raise even though they thought highly of the job he'd done.

I made calls and attended meetings, but all I was getting was frustrated. I got absolutely nowhere. Finally, because I was such a brilliant and astute negotiator, I was able to obtain a very substantial raise for the rabbi over a three-year period. How was I able to do this? *I* had to make the donation to the synagogue to pay for the raise to the rabbi! I have since decided that I don't care to represent any more clergyman.

The directors of the temple and the congregation were very pleased with the arrangement and allowed me to do it year after year. Ah, but the story didn't end there. What came next defined the word *chutzpah*— great gall or nerve. The year after the negotiation for my rabbi, a representative of the temple called me and said, "Look, we're thinking of letting the rabbi go. But if we do, can we count on you to still make your donation?" Thank goodness, my rabbi is still there.

Dealing for the "Tooz"

In my profession, where there is always a sensitivity to how the media will portray a situation, there are numerous ways to create leverage. One is to make sure the buyer can actually see how close he is to losing what he might have.

Back in 1973, I represented the late John Matuszak. At six-eight and 290 pounds, Big John (later known as "The Tooz") was one of the most ferocious, powerful, and unpredictable players in National Football League history.

John had been drafted by the lowly Houston Oilers, whose general manager, Sid Gillman, was one of the most creative football minds in the sport. But at the negotiating table, he was tough, moralistic, intransigent, and a tightwad. He believed that easy money corrupted players and he wasn't going to part with any money he didn't have to.

I got a letter from Gillman informing me of what the Oilers would pay for Matuszak. The letter said it was the team's first, best, and final offer. It was only for half of John's market value.

I responded to Gillman by phone. "Sid, I got your letter and I'd like to come down and talk about it."

"What's there to talk about?" Sid said. The phone slammed down.

Two months went by. We sat next to each other at a banquet where I said, "I'm sure if we just got together for a couple of hours, we could accomplish a lot on Matuszak."

"I haven't got the time," Sid replied.

I was frustrated. Sid didn't seem to care a whit about signing Matuszak. In the end, I sat tight. I had to be patient. I didn't know what to do.

Six weeks later, I was in Canada completing a contract for one of my hockey clients, Bob Gainey of the Montreal Canadiens. At a press conference for Gainey, a writer asked me how I was progressing with Matuszak. I said we had problems.

An hour later, I received an emergency call from the late John Bassett, then the owner of the Toronto Argonauts of the Canadian Football League. "Would your fellow be interested in playing up here? We have the rights to him in Canada and we'd love to get him."

I told Bassett that Matuszak would listen to any legitimate offer. Within twenty-four hours, John was in Toronto. His arrival was a media event, and photographs of the two of us strolling the downtown streets moved through the wire services and appeared prominently in Houston newspapers.

When I returned to my office in Houston, Sid Gillman was on the phone. He was warm and talkative, so unlike his previous demeanor. "Bobby," he said, "this is Sid. Why haven't we heard from you? We've got to get together. Why don't you come on down as soon as it's convenient and we'll get this business settled?"

Gillman knew the leverage had tilted the other way. He had to make a decision because the pressure was now on him to make a move. Within a day of my arrival in Houston, we made a deal. As I packed my briefcase I asked Gillman, "Sid, why did you put me through all of that?"

He smiled. "I send out fifty contracts every year," he said. "It works eight or nine times. I thought it was worth the shot."

Negotiators are constantly trying to create leverage when they can't do it from concrete strengths. They do it through their phrasing and their actions. They manufacture what they believe will change the psychological atmosphere.

Getting Leverage from the Media

When you or your client is in the public eye, don't ignore the media. They can seem like vultures circling for the kill. But they don't have to circle over *you*. Having them on your side can provide added leverage.

Unless you give the media cause to dislike you, they can be your allies. All they're looking for is a story, comment, and illumination. Most want to explore both sides of an issue. If you gain a reputation as someone who will be honest and available, you will almost always be treated fairly.

I've been dealing extensively with the media for over twenty-five years, and a good chunk of my time each day is devoted to talking about my clients to the press. Reporters around the country know that if I'm busy, I'll call back. If I can't say anything, they respect that. If I tell them anything, they know I'm telling the truth. By doing this, I've made their life easier. They have a correct story (from my point of view) and I have information I want known out in the open.

I gain leverage by floating trial balloons (a client is thinking of leaving his team, for example) that could help in my negotiations and sometimes smoke out the other side's intentions. I don't always get what I want out of it. Occasionally, a confidence is violated. Or something intended to be off-the-record goes on-the-record. But in nearly all cases, my availability has resulted in gaining, at minimum, more attention for my client, and, at maximum, enhanced leverage to bring to the bargaining table.

Many people who are rarely quoted frequently deal quietly with the media. Investment bankers, team owners, and politicians (even presidents) talk as background and off-the-record sources to reporters. They want their side of a story known or want to push initiatives they can't talk about publicly. Even the media-shy spend dearly to hire publicists to deal with the press.

You run into two major problems if you don't cooperate with the media. One, because there are two sides to every story, a reporter will go to your opponent if you don't cooperate. It will produce an incomplete and, perhaps, inaccurate story. You may then have to respond in anger or in panic. Two, if you duck the media, you will gain a reputation as someone with something to hide.

There are some people who can operate just fine if they don't deal with the media. Some executives, owners, and attorneys just ignore the press without any second thoughts. They have a very thick skin and are willing to risk getting bad press. But the temptation to deal with the media—where reporters are greater in number and more aggressive than ever before—is great if you or your client are public personalities.

You *can* run and hide from the media. You can probably survive without all those reporters calling at odd hours for comment. But if your business requires public contact, you can do your negotiating stance more good than harm if you make yourself an agreeable and open source of information. You have to seek an edge in everything you do. When you don't have strictly factual leverage, dealing deftly with the media can produce an advantage you didn't have before. You can use the media as a tool for the benefit of both you and the newspaper or television or radio station you're talking to.

Would Kelly Leave? Read All About It

By the time that Kelly Tripucka, now a forward with the NBA Charlotte Hornets, became a free agent following the expiration of his three-year contract with the Detroit Pistons, he had proven his detractors wrong. He had made the successful transition from Notre Dame to the pros, averaging over twenty-one points per game, with selections to the All-Star team and starring roles in the playoffs. At contract time, he was at the top of his market value.

Detroit's first offer was $600,000 a year. Then something strange occurred. The Pistons signed their superstar guard, Isiah Thomas, for $650,000 a year and *decreased* their offer to Tripucka to $400,000 a year. I was terribly disappointed that Detroit would take back one-third of an offer that was negotiated in good faith. Kelly's market value was much higher and we all knew it. The Pistons either didn't care about creating hard feelings or they were daring us to leave.

Kelly was a positive asset, a talented, hard-working, and articulate team player. I inquired around the league and found a receptive ear with Harry Weltman, then general manager of the Cleveland Cavaliers. The Cavaliers were a struggling but salvageable franchise, and a solid, popular, intelligent player like Tripucka might have been right for that team.

I wanted to establish a price so high that Detroit would not match the offer sheet the Cavaliers would tender to Kelly. At that time, Detroit had the right to match the offer of any other team. While Cleveland had no intention of throwing away money, they recognized the need to preempt the competition. We settled on a seven-year, $6.3 million deal, about half a million dollars per year more than the Pistons had offered.

But there was a catch: the owners of the Cavaliers and Pistons were close friends, and Cavaliers owner Ted Stepien told me, "I have absolutely no desire to hurt or upset my friend, Bill Davidson. If I sign Tripucka, he'll be extremely angry and I don't want to jeopardize our relationship by doing anything that might even remotely be construed as stealing one of his players. I will only sign Tripucka if Tripucka truly wants to leave Detroit. I must have proof positive that Kelly is dissatisfied, that he really wants to change teams. It needs to be a tangible statement, perhaps in a headline in the Detroit paper that says he wants out."

While I knew that Kelly wanted to stay in Detroit, I was also aware that he had been hurt by the Pistons' reduced offer. I felt that if I phrased the statement correctly I could meet Ted Stepien's conditions without jeopardizing Kelly's future with the Pistons, should he end up staying with them. Rather than have Kelly make statements which might be used against him in the future (such as whenever the Cavaliers played in Detroit), I decided to talk to the press myself. I had to be extremely careful about my language and the scope of my statement. The residual effects of a badly worded phrase could have been devastating.

"I am negotiating with the Detroit Pistons," I told the press, "but Kelly is very upset by the fact that they decreased their original offer to him and that they did not show faith in his abilities or his importance to the team.

"If the Pistons really do harbor these kinds of feelings for Kelly Tripucka, then he would prefer to play elsewhere."

I was very sure to begin that last phrase with the conditional "if," not "because." I was offering a proposition, not a threat. That was the key.

Well, the headline hit: "Tripucka Wants to Be Traded." As I watched headlines appear in the Detroit papers, I was aware that pressure was being applied on the Pistons and the Cavaliers. Detroit had played well in that year's playoffs and had a nucleus of young and talented ballplayers who, for the first time in many years, had a real chance to develop into a generation of title contenders. The fans, who were finally getting interested in the team after years of apathy, might revolt if such a promising team were dismantled over a contract dispute. The Pistons had to decide whether the dollars saved were worth the risk of undermining the franchise. The Cavaliers, on the other hand, had given their word that they would make their offer if certain conditions were met, and we had met them fully.

Cleveland, as they had promised, extended their $6.3 million offer to Kelly and expected to get Kelly unchallenged. I was quite surprised when Detroit matched the offer and kept him. I believe the Pistons' management had been influenced, embarrassed, and swayed by the pressure of the hometown headlines. It took a bit of gamesmanship and a careful use of language, but by creating pressure where there had been none, we had more than doubled Kelly Tripucka's salary.

Part Two

101 PROVEN TACTICS, TECHNIQUES, AND STRATEGIES

CHAPTER SEVEN

What to Do Before the Negotiation

"Better ask twice than go wrong once."
—ANONYMOUS

YOU'RE NOW ready to begin the negotiation. You've done your research, prepared your facts, and thought about how you'll be presenting your case. The following 101 points will remind you of the things I want you to be aware of throughout the entire negotiating process. I'll show you how important it is to control your emotions in the course of a negotiation, as well as review the techniques and strategies that you will use to complete your negotiations successfully.

I want you to be prepared for the give-and-take of a real negotiation and the crucial strategic nuances that may make or break your agreement. You ought to know how to set the right tempo in a negotiation and maintain a positive attitude throughout, even when it looks as if talks aren't going your way. You should establish realistic goals and be prepared to ignore tactics meant to intimidate. I want you to be prepared for every development, from deciding where and when to negotiate, to being sure not to gloat about your success.

This first section deals with a variety of points you'll want to keep in mind before formal talks begin.

1. Should You Negotiate by Telephone or in Person?

Most negotiations are multimedia events, conducted in part by telephone, in part by personal contact, and some by correspondence. Trust your instincts. Go with your abilities. Try to communicate through the means you feel are most advantageous to your style.

Each person should evaluate his or her own style and ability on the telephone. Some people are more effective on the phone. Others are more effective in person. Some get flustered in face-to-face encounters, but can maintain a confident manner while on the phone. Some people have a commanding telephone voice. Through voice alone they can be as persuasive in negotiations as silver-throated radio disc jockeys can be soothing to listeners.

While many people find that most of their negotiations or business transactions are over the telephone, sometimes the type of negotiation will determine the method of communication. If you buy a stock, you use the phone. If you want a car, you will communicate face-to-face. Where you and the other side are located may also limit your communications options. If you are many miles apart, the odds are you will at least have to start your talks by phone.

Once you get to know your opponent you may not find face-to-face meetings necessary. Travel alone can take up a lot of time that can be spent negotiating by phone.

2. If Negotiating by Phone—Be the Caller

If you are negotiating by phone, you should be the caller. If they call you, you may not be fully prepared. The files may not be in front of you. Your research may not be complete. You may not be emotionally "up" for the conversation at that moment. Your first reaction is "What am I going to say?" Gain the advantage: be the caller.

I always prefer to do the calling. I let the other person be the one who isn't prepared and has to catch up with me. If someone calls me unexpectedly wanting to negotiate, I will say, "Let me get back to you."

Make the call when *you* are prepared, in the right frame of mind and when your adrenalin is pumping.

3. If in Person, Always Try to Negotiate in Your Office

Whenever possible, when negotiations move into an office, I want it to be mine. The reason is as simple as the home court advantage in sports. I know where things are. I can control the distractions. I have my own people and my own files around me. I'm more comfortable on my own turf.

It is no fluke that teams usually play their best at home. It is a proven psychological edge. Boston Garden is one of the premier home courts in sports where visiting teams feel the Celtics' history and success hanging in the air as surely as they see the NBA championship banners hanging from the rafters. Year after year, the Celtics win far more than they lose on their familiar parquet floor.

If your offices happen to be in different cities, or on different coasts, who travels where may give you a reading on how the negotiation will go. If the other party lives in Los Angeles and you're in Boston, and he's coming to *you*, then you can assume he will not fly 3,000 miles to return empty-handed. He is coming to make a deal.

4. Almost Everything Is Negotiable

Before you ever walk in the door, utter a single word to the other side or mail the first letter, your attitude should be that almost everything is negotiable. Experience has shown me that no matter what people say or do—they won't sell or they won't buy—through a little creative persuasion you can get them at least to consider, or reconsider, just about anything.

There is no situation where the circumstances can't be changed to create a potentially successful negotiation. If a buyer offered a million dollars for that house you said you'd never sell, would you reconsider? No? Two million? Still no? Two million plus stock in the buyer's company?

Do you think the prices at the department store are not negotiable? *"This suit has an imperfection, I'll buy it for 30 percent off the list price."* *"There's a stain on this dress, I'll take it off your hands for half-price."* You think you can't get prices off at the furniture store? *"This dining room table is scratched, but I'll take it if you take seventy-five dollars off."*

Almost no matter what the situation is, you *can* find a way to bring the other side to the negotiating table. It takes a keen eye, a creative mind, good listening, and sharp questions to elicit the opening you may need to persuade the other side that common ground and mutual interest actually do exist.

5. Predetermine the Tempo of the Negotiation

Before you start, whether you are buying or selling, you should try to look at all the factors that will be coming up in the future that can affect the negotiations. Negotiations are rarely, if ever, concluded in one conversation or one meeting. If you buy a house, or a car or a company, a series of meetings may be involved.

How often do you want to meet? How much do you want to accomplish at each meeting? Will your schedule allow a quick succession of meetings? Will your opponent's? You can control the pace if you know your own strong and weak points. You should try to predetermine if it is to your advantage to move quickly or slowly. Moving slowly may force your opponent to adjust his tempo (and perhaps what he wants) if he perceives by your pace that you don't seem to *need* his product or service. However, if both sides face the end of a contract and a strike is imminent, you may have to move quickly.

A lot will depend on what the other side says to you. Sometimes, I'm pleasantly surprised that the other side wants to get things done quickly. Have a game plan for the tempo of the meetings. You can always adjust it.

6. Timing: Negotiate When You Look Good

People reward quality. If you have just set a company sales record, or won the Nobel Prize, don't wait to be noticed. Step forward and ask for what you want. Not later. Now.

Don't be sidetracked by modesty. Don't assume that because you have done well you will receive whatever your heart desires. Your goals may not be known to the people in a position to reward you. Your standing will never be higher than when you are basking in the spotlight of achievement. In that time and spirit you should decide what you want and go after it.

Randy Vataha came out of Stanford University as a last-round draft pick with slim chances of making it in the NFL. At five-nine and 170 pounds, he had spent one college vacation playing one of Snow White's seven dwarfs at Disneyland. He was dropped by the Los Angeles Rams before the start of the regular season and waived by every club until Jim Plunkett, then the New England Patriots' quarterback, convinced his bosses to give his former Stanford teammate a tryout. Vataha signed a one-year contract.

From the start, Randy was an astounding success for the Patriots and by season's end, had broken three of the team's all-time receiving records. In the final game, he caught an eighty-eight-yard touchdown pass from Plunkett to knock the Baltimore Colts out of first place in the division.

The next day, I went to the Patriots' offices and negotiated a substantially improved contract for him. The team was not necessarily in any hurry to reward Randy or look to his future. But the mood and timing were in his favor and he received a contract that better reflected his success on the field. In short, we struck while he was looking good.

On the other hand, it isn't a good idea to negotiate when you look bad. This may seem like an obvious statement, but you would be amazed how often it is overlooked. When things aren't going well, desperation may set in. It is unpleasant and it can cloud your judgment. You may feel you need security when times are darkest, but only two things can happen, both of them bad.

First, because your market value is decreased and your prospects uncertain, you may be turned down cold, a devastating result. Second, because your leverage is low and your needs high, you may get an offer well below your fair market value and you might be tempted to accept it. It is best just to bite the bullet and work in other areas to salvage your situation. For instance, it is not the ideal time for a broker to press his client for more business when a stock that the broker has touted to a client has fallen like a marble down a drainpipe. Instead, the broker would better serve his future dealings by tending to the other holdings of his client to contain any further losses.

Common sense should tell you when to promote yourself or your cause when conditions are in your favor and when to lie low when they are not.

7. Timing: Negotiate When the Other Side Is Happy

It may sound elementary to say that there are good and bad times for your opponents to talk business. However, this is another overlooked aspect of negotiating.

A telephone call to offer congratulations can easily turn into a productive business conversation. It is natural for people to feel expansive when things are going well for them. By applauding or sharing in the other person's success, you may establish a smoother and more amicable relationship than the one you had when the day began. This is a timeless business and social practice. In the movie *The Godfather* you may recall that Don Corleone (played by Marlon Brando) granted one request to anyone who petitioned him on his special day of joy, the occasion of his daughter's wedding.

By the same token, if a company has just enjoyed its most productive quarter, the time could hardly be more ripe to approach management about a job, a contract, or a merger. A good negotiator knows who is having those happy days and why, and he will make a point of being alert to these more advantageous times to negotiate.

A good negotiator will also know when it is *not* the best time to make contact with the other side. If the other person is experiencing the recent loss of a loved one or a disaster in his business, he most probably won't be in the frame of mind to hear you out, so try to wait until he is in a better position to think about your proposal.

One of my clients was an actor on a popular television series. On the day after one of his co-stars suddenly died, he called and asked that I contact the producers to have his name moved up to replace that of the deceased in the show's order of credits. I was appalled. I told my client I would not even consider such a request. Not only was it in very poor taste, but the only outcome would be to discredit himself in the television industry. The death was a cause for mourning, not career advancement. People felt bad enough without someone using the tragedy to jockey for a better position.

Be sensitive to the other side's position in order to take advantage of any weaknesses, but don't ever lose sight of having compassion for them as well.

8. One-Shot Deals

You will often be in a negotiation where you believe you will never run across that person again. There may be a temptation to subscribe to an idea some experts encourage; that you can treat them in a demeaning and intimidating fashion because you won't have to face them again. That is not what my years of experience tell me. You will wind up with just as much, or more, if you follow the same principles of any other negotiation and treat them with respect.

And how can you be absolutely certain that you will never run across that person in the future, or their family or friends or colleagues? People who have been abused tend to have long memories. My bottom line is this: there are never any good reasons to mistreat anyone.

9. Don't Get Discouraged

One day, I went into the office and everything went wrong. Every piece of mail seemed to bring bad news. Every phone call brought more aggravation. Around noon, I said to heck with it. I'm going to spend the rest of the day playing golf.

I went out to the golf course and got struck by lightning.

So don't get discouraged. Things can always get worse. Negotiation is a process, not a simple transaction. There are going to be ups and downs, unexpected problems, maybe newfound opportunities, and very often, changes. This may well be a long process, so remember this at the onset and be prepared for these detours and potholes.

Don't think that the results you want will come freely or easily. You are going to have to work for them, and before you go into the negotiation keep this in mind, so that when problems arise or when you hit an impasse, you are ready. Instead of getting discouraged at such times, you will be prepared for them, and this preparation will give you added strength to continue instead of stopping.

Rarely have I been through a negotiation where my heart hasn't sunk to my stomach when I thought the deal was completely falling apart. But I know from experience that this is going to happen. At some point, it will always look as though you can't make a deal for what you think is fair. But I also know that the majority of the time, the negotiation will be successful.

When you're discouraged is the time to stay cool and be your most creative. Keep reassessing the situation. Try to see the holes and the opportunities. Determine *what* is discouraging you; don't analyze your frustrated feelings.

10. It Doesn't Hurt to Ask

I've mentioned this concept several times already, but it bears repeating. If there is one thing I've learned about human nature, it is that most people hate to ask for what they want. They can be brilliant or successful or rich and they can still be afraid to ask. It isn't that what they are asking for is outrageous or unreasonable. They are usually fearful of confrontation or having others think they are greedy, pushy, or offensive. Sometimes, they flat out forget to ask. If you don't ask, you won't know what the other side might be willing to give you. You won't even know if they'd be happy to give something to you—if only you'd asked.

The number one rule in sales is that you have to ask for the order. You may give the most brilliant presentation, but don't expect a deal to be consummated unless you *ask* for it. Thomas "Tip" O'Neill was used to asking people for their votes all his public life. Not only could he ask, he could cajole and exhibit his friendly brand of persuasion. But as he writes in his autobiography, during his campaign for Cambridge City

Council, he learned a lesson from his high school drama-and-elocution teacher.

As Tip recalls it, on the night before the election, Mrs. O'Brien said to him, "Tip, I'm going to vote for you tomorrow even though you didn't ask me to."

Tip was shocked. "Why, Mrs. O'Brien, I've lived across from you for eighteen years. I cut your grass in the summer. I shovel your walk in the winter. I didn't think I had to ask for your vote."

"Tip," she replied, "let me tell you something: people like to be asked."

O'Neill lost that election, his only electoral loss. There's no telling if he might have won if he'd just *asked* for more votes from people he assumed were in his corner.

People who are afraid or unwilling to ask for what they want or need are often disappointed, and settle for less than they should. Believe me, you should ask for anything so long as it is practical and not totally divorced from reality. It isn't *what* you ask for, but *how* you ask that is the key here. As long as you ask in a civil and inoffensive way, you won't be hurt. You never know when you will get some or all of what you seek.

A confrontation can always be avoided by not asking for a raise, or by undervaluing yourself, settling for less than you deserve. The difference between what you want and what you get is the price you pay for your fear of asking.

You can ask for anything if you ask in the proper way. Be creative. Say, "Does a car go with this job?" not, "I want a car." Say, "Does the price of the house include the furnishings?" not, "For this price, the furnishings better come with the house."

Ask in a questioning way, not a demanding way. This is where you put into action your "style"; how you present your request is critical. The more polished your style is, the less likely you are to have a fear of confrontation. Ask and you *may* receive. Don't ask, and you can be sure you won't.

Sometimes you will be pleasantly surprised when you ask. When the contract of Bruce Williams, the well-known network radio talk show host, was up for renewal, I asked for an exceptionally high annual salary that I thought NBC Radio certainly wouldn't meet. But they came back to me and said, "Fine." Unbeknownst to me and to everyone else, since it was extremely confidential news known only to the NBC and Westwood One principals, NBC was selling off its radio network to Westwood One and Williams was a key asset in the deal. Without Williams under contract, the agreement might have collapsed, or at least been heavily rewritten to NBC's disadvantage. Thus, if I hadn't asked, I never would have received the higher salary from NBC.

When all is said and done, all you risk from asking is being told one simple word: "no." But you'll never know if that word could have been "yes," if you don't *ask*.

11. Be Aware of Your Goals

All through the negotiation, you should keep reminding yourself of what you were originally trying to accomplish. This is necessary to keep you from getting caught up in fringe or emotional issues or allowing yourself to be sidetracked by the creative arguments of the other side.

Never underestimate the other side. He or she might be a good salesman, convincing or clever. Don't be like the fellow who went car shopping for a Chevrolet and came home with a Mercedes. He may have gotten a great buy on it, but that wasn't what he set out to do, which was buy a nice secondhand car for his teenage children to drive.

By being aware of your goals from the start (write them down if doing so will help you return to them) and rechecking them with steady regularity, you can always assess how far away you are getting from them.

12. Keep an Eye on the Bottom Line

A negotiation can be a very emotional experience. You may want something to happen badly, and someone is standing in your way. In the emotionalism of the moment, you never want to lose sight of what you have determined is *not* a good deal for you or your client. Throughout negotiations you should reassess your bottom line and determine where you are in relation to it.

If you are ever going to change your bottom line, and there are times when you might, this should be done calmly, with patience and deliberate thought. Let me define the bottom line: this is the last line of resistance, the point below which it is no longer practical to go through with the deal.

An example that comes into mind is that of the vacationer who goes to Las Vegas, telling himself he won't lose more than $500. Period. Tops. Then he gets caught up in the excitement, passes the $500 mark without slowing down, and the next thing he knows, he's in the hole for a thousand or more. If he had stopped at $500 and decided to sleep on it, chances are that he might have stayed away from the tables.

13. Don't Be Intimidated Just Because It's Printed

People are intimidated by what they assume to be the power of legitimacy. They don't believe they can challenge anything that is in writing, whether it is in a contract or on a sign. If it seems to be a *policy*, some people believe it is unshakeable, holy writ. They get intimidated just because it's in print.

The hotel desk says you *must* check out by noon. (You can usually get late checkout for an hour or two later.)

You are handed a rate card or price list. (If you sign a long-term contract or buy in volume, you get a discount.)

The menu says no substitutions. (If you pay a few dollars more, the rule quickly fades away.)

Your lease doesn't allow a pet. (Does that mean you kill your canary? Does "pet" mean just a dog or cat?)

The printed price on a price tag doesn't mean that has to be the price. (Is there a special sale going on? If you buy two will you get a reduced price? If it's still there when you come back in two weeks, can you get a discount?)

Does the fact that these are printed documents mean they are not negotiable? Of course not. I will say it again: *everything* is negotiable.

Don't be intimidated by the printed word, by standard contracts or leases. Such texts are printed and delivered in such a way as to guide you into working with them. This is how *they* want things done, not local law. They've had their office or their lawyer draw up the contract. This is how *they* work. Fine. It's not how you work. They are trying to use peer pressure at the negotiating level. The implication is simply, "Well, everyone else uses this lease, I guess I should not object." At the very least, raise questions.

14. Proper Timing in Breaking Bad News

As with any information in a negotiation, the best time to break bad news is when it will have the least negative effect. My executive vice president, Jill Leone, routinely withholds information from me during a workday if she thinks it will upset me and prevent me from accomplishing the other things I need to do.

Bad news will catch up to you and unless it needs to be handled immediately, such as a family death or a major disaster, it is just as well left for the moment when it will cause less damage. There is a lot to be said for selective protection.

Jill used her good judgment in temporarily withholding news from Doug Flutie, for example. Doug and his wife, Laurie, were in New York City, where he was taping an English Leather television commercial on the day the merger between the USFL New Jersey Generals and Houston Gamblers became public. They had been up at daybreak and were in the closed environment of a television studio session when the Generals released the information that Doug would no longer be the Generals' starting quarterback because of the merger.

Jill was notified on the set and could have told Doug immediately, but she realized that Doug would have been unsettled, his enthusiasm dampened and the commercial, due to be seen for months all over the network TV schedule, would inevitably have suffered. The commercial was one of Doug's entrees into the mass media market and he needed to be at his best.

Under the circumstances, Jill decided that this piece of news could wait, and I supported her judgment. That evening, after the television taping was completed, she told Doug what had happened. He was upset, as expected, but his disappointment was contained to a more private setting and not transmitted over the airwaves to millions of viewers.

15. Some of the Best Moves Are the Ones You Don't Make

Some of my best deals, and investments, *were the ones I didn't make*. Sometimes, the very best way to double your money is to fold it over twice and put it back in your wallet. In his song "The Gambler" Kenny Rogers sings, "know when to hold them and know when to fold them." There's many a negotiation that just wasn't meant to be, so recognize this fact and have the courage to walk away. I can't tell you the countless business "opportunities" I've walked away from because they just didn't seem fair and in retrospect, I'm glad that I did. But of course, in business matters, I am extremely conservative. I belong to the Will Rogers School of finance: I am more concerned with the return *of* my investment, than a return *on* my investment. But, in general, you will find that there are times when if you don't feel right about the deal, it's because you shouldn't be making it.

16. Don't Take Anything Personally

Most of what is said in negotiating is said to gain a specific advantage. If there is an attempt being made to insult you, most of the time it is just to distract you from your goal. The other side could well use the same lines on the next person with whom they deal. It is "shop talk," nothing else. Just put some space between yourself and your positions. The attacks are on what you seek, not who you are.

The world is filled with unenlightened people who will try to browbeat, abuse, or insult you. If they are being unpleasant, maybe something else is going on in their lives that has carried over into your dealings. Always try to separate the issues from the person. In short, do not overreact. You have to understand temperament: who angers quickly and who doesn't; who carries a grudge and who drops it off at the first stop.

I once sent a letter to a team general manager with preliminary salary requests for a basketball player I represent. The reply that came back said:

"Dear Bob,

Hahahahahahahahahahahahahaha!"

If I didn't know who it was coming from—an unorthodox, jocular NBA general manager—I'd have been upset. But I had to slough it off. That's the way the man is. So I tossed his note in the circular file and went ahead with the negotiation, and ended up getting what I was looking for.

17. It Never Works for One Negotiator to Insult Another's Intelligence

There was one slight hitch in my negotiations with the New England Patriots on behalf of Gerard Phelan, the Boston College wide receiver who caught Doug Flutie's "Miracle Pass" against the University of Miami. The money had come up short on the third year of a contract offered by their general manager, Pat Sullivan.

A hometown hero, Phelan had been drafted on the fourth round. He was a popular choice for them. Boston College had captured the city's heart in the Flutie era, while the Patriots had been less than competitive in recent seasons. With Flutie headed for the USFL, the Patriots would score points by keeping half the magic act at home.

Phelan was talented and hardworking with a knack for being in the right place. On Flutie's last-second pass, Gerard lost sight of the ball in the haze and lights of the Orange Bowl as he streaked for the end zone. All of a sudden, a patch of clear air opened and there was the ball. It was not until the team had moved its celebration into the locker room that Flutie learned who had caught the ball—his best friend and roommate.

The talks with New England had been relatively smooth. Sullivan had offered an $85,000 signing bonus and a three-year contract, with the third year at $140,000. When I left on a trip to Israel, we talked by overseas telephone. I kept saying, "Pat, you have to do something on the third year. If you can do a little better, then we've got a deal."

Finally, Sullivan said, "I'll tell you what. I'll take $10,000 off the signing bonus and we'll put it on the third year's salary."

It was like watching an illusionist do his card tricks, urging you to notice that at no time do his fingers ever leave his hand. Pat had, in effect, offered to take $10,000 out of Phelan's pocket, let the team hold it for three years and then give it back to him. Not only was there no gain on the third year, we would lose both capital and interest and the use of the money for investment purposes.

More to the point, the contract wasn't even guaranteed, meaning that Phelan might never see the money downstream. I held my temper— I was in the Holy Land, after all—but I was more determined than ever to improve upon the contract with the Patriots. Having gotten to the lip of the cup, I felt the club was now being capricious with us.

The proposal was so absurd that I thought Sullivan was joking, but he wasn't. Sullivan was hoping to get it by me. The tactic did not improve their position and pushed us farther apart. By making a ridiculous offer, the Patriots delayed Gerard's signing, which hurt the team and Gerard as a player, and gained nothing. We held the line, and, ultimately, Phelan signed a three-year contract that was more in his favor and met all our goals.

18. Establish Realistic Goals

Before you start the negotiating process, you should make sure that from your research you have produced a fair and reasonable proposal. You need to be honest with yourself up front. If you have realistic goals and realistic numbers, you are less likely to weaken as the negotiation drags on. If your bottom line is competitive it will keep the other side interested in making an agreement with you. If your terms are unrealistic you will be setting yourself up for failure, so don't become your own worst enemy in a negotiation.

CHAPTER EIGHT

What to Do During the Negotiation

"Never promise more than you can perform."

—PUBLILIUS SYRUS

"The surest way to knock the chip off a fellow's shoulder is by patting him on the back."

—ANONYMOUS

IT'S TIME to start the talks. How *do* you start? What do you do? Remember, it's never as difficult as you think. You're prepared. You know how to conduct yourself so the atmosphere is appropriate. You know how to treat the other side. You know your goals and what you need to attain all or most of them.

So now the pre-game warm-ups are over; it's time to run out onto the field. I'm going to take you through the game, play by play from what you say to start the ball rolling right through how to treat your negotiating partner after you get what you want.

Now visualize the scene: you're on the phone. You're in that conference room. It's time to negotiate.

19. Begin the Conversation with Pleasantries

More often than not two people will sit down to begin a negotiation and they will be nervous. In order to help relieve the tension, start out your negotiation process with some small talk. You should always let the other person feel good about talking to you. So don't just walk in and start negotiating. Don't start off by announcing, "Let's get on with this immediately." This is the time to humanize yourself.

No matter how difficult you think the negotiation may be, you need to develop a friendly rapport. You've seen diplomats on the evening news coming out of five hours of talks. Well, about three hours of those talks were spent on trying to establish a rapport, telling personal stories about their families, necessary preludes to actual negotiating.

So when you're starting, admire that family photograph on the desk or wall. There's no better place to start. How old are the children? In or out of school? How about the person's college ring? Can you find something to relate to his or her alma mater? Talk about the news. Talk about sports. Whatever seems appropriate to take the ensuing negotiation to a friendly, pleasant plane.

Showing a personal interest is not only good manners; you may learn a nugget of information that you can use later, either to lighten up a dark moment or alter the agreement to your liking. You may also find that you have common interests which will make negotiating more pleasant.

20. Re-create the Atmosphere

In chapter 2, I pointed out the advantage of trying to set up the right atmosphere in which to negotiate. This is an extension of personalizing the situation. Now you have to show the person on the other side of the table that you're prepared to recreate and continue the atmosphere you've set previously. You're putting a personal stamp on your reputation and positive attitude. It's your first chance to let the other side see you at work as well as to reduce his anxiety. You want to assure the other person that your goal in the negotiation is not to outsmart, hurt, or berate him. Your mind is open. You want to make a deal that will benefit both of you.

Now you're face-to-face with the person you may have possibly dealt with only by telephone. You've got a chance to be forthright, candid, and reassuring. I try to be very encouraging, saying things like, "We *will* make a deal" and "I'm glad we're here and we will get through this, *no matter* how difficult it may get." Or, "I'm only looking for what's fair" and "I would like you to know that I'm here in good faith and I hope you feel the same way."

21. Try to Get the Other Side to Make the First Offer

I've found that I never want to make the first offer. You want to know what's on their mind before they find out what's on yours. You always want to be in the position of getting information before you give it.

If you can get them to go first—and you won't always succeed—you may find that you've made some false assumptions about what you thought they'd offer. Even if you don't get a firm dollar offer, it makes sense to let them go first. The opportunity is there to gain valuable information that may cause you to alter your counteroffer. You may learn why they made their proposal or took their position. And what have you told them so far? Very little, I hope. It isn't all that difficult to get the other side talking first.

You can ask, "What's in your budget?" "What are you thinking?" "What did you have in mind?" or "Please give me some ideas of what you can offer or what you feel comfortable with."

Making the first offer without full knowledge of the situation you're talking about can turn out disastrously. Just ask the Beatles. Their manager, Brian Epstein, came out of the retail furniture business. He had some background in music, and a good business sense, which he used to negotiate many successful deals that made the four Liverpuddlians very wealthy men. He did, however, have at least one major fiasco, which occurred because he was in unfamiliar territory and never got the appropriate information before negotiating for the Fab Four.

In the autumn of 1963, the Beatles were a British success but had not yet arrived in the United States. They did not know whether they would ever be more than a big band on a little island, and the opportunity to make a movie was a large step forward at that early stage of their career.

Epstein was approached by a producer, who, with the financial backing of United Artists Pictures, had envisioned the project as a teenage exploitation movie and had budgeted accordingly, at $300,000. The two men and a United Artists executive met to discuss the deal. To appear in the film, the Beatles were offered $25,000 plus a percentage of the profits. Because of the film's low budget and modest expectations, the producer and film executive were prepared to offer Epstein and the Beatles up to 25 percent of the profits. They asked Epstein to tell them what he wanted. Epstein, not intimate with the movie business or its standards, and having made minimal efforts to find out what would be an appropriate cut for the Beatles, said, "I wouldn't accept anything less than 7.5 percent." Not only did he make the mistake of going first with his proposal instead of waiting to hear the other side's offer, he was misinformed as to the norm of getting paid higher percentages of a profit when the movie's low budget prevented higher cash advances to the talent.

Unfortunately for the Beatles, at least from a financial point of view, the film was *A Hard Day's Night*, which grossed millions of dollars. The Beatles received considerably less of that money than they could have because Brian Epstein made the crucial mistake of being underinformed and going first.

22. Don't Get Angry Because the Offer Isn't What You Wanted

A lot of people get upset when the first offer on the table isn't what they wanted. And they get visibly angry because the terms aren't what they want to hear. Even with my years of experience, I get an inner twinge of anger and annoyance when a proposal isn't what I'd hoped for.

But get openly angry? Forget it. Don't take it so seriously. It's only the *first* offer and you haven't even stepped up to the plate yet. So hide your emotion. Remember, your opponent is merely starting the process. Just because the offer isn't what you had hoped for, don't tell the other person that his proposal is an insult. He's *not* trying to insult you. He's doing his job. So don't get disturbed by it. You'll have your chance to counter his proposal. And when that moment comes, you won't want to be the subject of *his* anger.

Stay in control. Anger is not a quality emotion and will not pave the way for a good negotiation, especially if your veins pop at the first offer.

23. A Negotiation Doesn't Have To Be a Long, Drawn-Out Procedure

Sometimes you will encounter someone who wants to come to an agreement as quickly as possible. He will immediately give you a fair and equitable offer in order to complete the agreement so he can move on to his next order of business with someone else. Don't be afraid to come to an agreement quickly. If you have done your homework you will be able to recognize when you have an excellent offer on the table. Just because the agreement transpired quickly does not mean it was a poor negotiation on your part. Don't be avaricious and greedy because sometimes you will have overstepped your boundaries and this type of person will take his offer away as quickly as he made it.

24. Keep Inquiring

You've learned the value of information in your preparation. But throughout the negotiation, you must keep fixed in your mind how important it is to keep gathering new information and jump at every opportunity to do so. Based on what the other side has told you about his first offer, there may be questions you want to ask for more information or clarification of his position and this is the time to ask.

Your opponent's first offer is your first chance to gather more information. You've heard what he's had to say, and before you reveal what you will propose, ask questions. Don't be overwhelming. But the more and better your information, the more clearly you can interpret and adjust your proposal. Information will help you make the best decisions.

Don't expect the other person to address every point in his written proposal. There may be smaller issues that could be addressed by asking questions whereby you can elicit information that can prove helpful throughout your talks.

25. Determine How Much Room He Has to Move

When someone makes a proposal, it will generally contain several points: the amount of money, the number of years, whether it is guaranteed or not. Some points will be more important than others. Before you get back to him with a counterproposal, you want to ascertain what he really needs and what is optional.

You may be offered a five-year contract for you or your client. My response is, "Does it have to be five? Could it be two years or three?" Maybe the length of the contract isn't all that important and the five-year proposal was just an opening gambit. Try to evaluate his priorities and what he *really* needs.

When I hear the terms of an offer, I always say, "Is this in cement?" just to find out what is important and what's not. Before I utter a syllable regarding what I want, I'm trying to find out the leeway I have; where I can expand it.

26. Try to Assess His Weaknesses

In addition to discovering your negotiating partner's needs through his presentation and your questions, you can also discover a weakness that might have been unknown to you. Is there pressure to close a deal by Friday? Is there only one in town of whatever he is looking for, and do you own or represent it? Does he have to leave by a certain time? Is this a deal your opponent *must* make and might determine a promotion?

Many people will accidentally reveal a weakness in answer to a question. If you sense a weakness, keep probing gently. Remember, you haven't made your presentation yet, so try to avoid giving any answers that might reveal *your* weaknesses.

27. Assess Your Leverage

This is, of course, something you will continue to do throughout the negotiation. But this is the first time in the negotiations that you'll go through this exercise. At this point, you'll have the information from the other side. You'll have analyzed it. You'll have decided what it means. Now you need to check your conclusions against what you originally thought were your points of leverage. Maybe you have gained some, lost some, any of which may alter your proposal.

You have to assess and reassess everything you've heard throughout the negotiation. This is an ongoing process.

28. Recheck His Authority and Decision-making Power

In your preparation, you've already sought to find out if this person can start and complete the deal. You've done that as a matter of course. Now's the time to find out in person if your opponent truly can go the distance. Many times I've started negotiations with the person who first contacted me only to discover that this person had little or no authority at all. It is appropriate—and not insulting—to ask at this point, "If we agree on terms, do you have the authority to make the deal?" or "Is there a point where you will have to consult others to complete the deal?" Sometimes going up the ladder of authority is inherent in a company. One executive may have authority to a certain dollar level, after which a superior must step in.

There will be times when you sense that your adversary may not want to admit his lack of authority. He may be waffling and noncommittal. When that happens, you may have to directly ask to move up the authority ladder. You should not say, "I'm going to talk to the CEO," but instead be conciliatory; "If you recommend that this be approved, will your boss agree?" That may give your opponent the opening to admit that he needs the okay from above and will turn the negotiation over to his superior.

29. I'll Get Back To You

If you have done a good job on everything up to this point, you have asked a lot of questions and gained a lot of new insights. You know what is behind their offer and at least some of what they are thinking.

I have learned from my experiences that I need time to absorb this information and analyze it. Exactly what did they tell me in their proposal? After I have received the proposal and asked all the questions, my standard reaction is to say, "Okay, let me give it some thought and consideration. I want to be sure I understand everything you told me. And I'll get back to you in a reasonable amount of time."

This gives you time to think it through and organize what you ought to say based on what he has told you. Even though you thought you were fully prepared, this review might prompt several changes in your presentation. This is especially important when negotiating on the telephone. You may not know what to say immediately, but you will be ready to reply in a few hours, a day or a week.

Of course, even when you want some time to reply, you have to show consideration. If someone has come several thousand miles to negotiate with you, you can't say, "I'll get back to you in three days." At best, you can ask for a few hours or the next day before making your proposal. But *always* seek some time to think about what you've heard.

The key is to avoid making snap decisions. Sometimes you will want to reply quickly when the agreement is fairly simple and extensive give-and-take is not necessary. But if you feel hesitant about replying and you feel you'll have to alter your proposal, you should wait before giving an answer. You'll get back to them.

30. Try to Reduce Their Expectations

Before making your presentation, keep in mind that it is critical to reduce the other side's expectations. The reasons are clear: you don't want your opponent to think you have *everything* he wants from you or that you won't easily agree to what he is offering you. You want the other person to think twice, and deflate his hopes.

The language that works best for me goes like this: "I hear what you are saying, but that isn't at all what I had in mind." Or, "I find what you have to say interesting, but it really doesn't address our needs." The idea is to bring down his level of expectation before you get into any of your specific numbers. You don't want him to feel he has a "live one," ready to jump at anything he's willing to offer.

Other verbal methods to reduce expectations: If you're the seller of a product or service, you can simply say, "Unfortunately, that's not competitive with market value," after you've heard an initial lowball offer. "This is what I have in mind."

If you're the buyer, it is appropriate to say, "What you are saying is not outrageous, but it isn't in my budget."

31. Make Your Presentation Logically

Now, for the first time, you are going to tell them what is on *your* mind. Make your proposal in a clear and concise way. No long speeches or crude jokes. Make it in a logical order from the most important point on down. There should be continuity to what you want to say. Make sense. Don't compare third basemen to wide receivers, or computer software to office furniture.

Start your case factually and sensibly: "This is what I had in mind," and tick off your points. By having heard the other side first, you've adjusted some of your points as you deem necessary. If your opponent's offer has given in to what you want, you can make known that you have a point of agreement, which should encourage your negotiating partner. But be concise, no after-dinner speeches. You are there to make an agreement, not compete in an oration contest.

If you're just starting out in a negotiation, you'll find it helpful to write your presentation down and try it out on colleagues, friends, or family. Even if you're alone, recite it aloud, so you can gain a rhythm and a sense of whether it makes logical sense. You'd be surprised how much of a difference it is to hear your words spoken and how much it will help in arranging your presentation.

In making your presentation, you can have it laid out on index cards. But it's more impressive to know it by heart. It shows you're prepared and polished.

32. Start High but Don't Be Ridiculous

You should absolutely start as high as you can in your requests, at figures you can *justify*. A number of studies have shown that if you start reasonably high, you are more likely to end up on the high side. If you start low, that is where you will usually finish. This applies not only to the money, but to every issue. If you are on the selling end, start high and if you are on the buying end, start as low as you can.

There is a natural fear that by opening with a high number you may anger or offend the other side and endanger the deal. Nonsense. As long as your figures can be justified, there is no reason for anyone to resent you for asking, even if they reject it out-of-hand.

This strategy applies to whether you go first or second in presenting your offer. If you go first, you're out there alone. You don't know if your offer might *seem* ridiculous because you haven't heard theirs. If you go second, you'll know what value the other side is putting on what you have, and you can raise the ante if it's appropriate to do so.

In starting at the highest level possible, you provide yourself with room to move and put yourself in a better position to be able to compromise without jeopardizing your bottom line.

33. Tell Him Your Unique Problem

You want the other person to sympathize with *you* and feel comfortable as he negotiates with you. One technique is to tell him your unique problem, if you have one. Instantly, you accomplish two things. You have shown your human side and taken him into your confidence. In effect, you have made him your accomplice. It's rare when the other side doesn't respond to your feeling this confidence in him, and he'll often drop a few hints about his problems.

You can tell the person with whom you're negotiating that your client is getting pressures within the family that affect the way you have to make your proposal. It doesn't weaken your case and it does show the other party that you are willing to trust him. But be cautious: don't give up any information that can hurt your leverage.

There can be any number of other unique problems besides family problems. There can be legitimate scheduling, timing, and financial constraints that can affect a negotiation. By confiding them to your adversary, you might also achieve another goal by reducing his expectations.

In return for my trusting the other side with these confidences, I've heard team and corporate executives moan about an owner or a boss giving them grief and how much they need to complete this deal successfully.

People want to be trusted. I want to be perceived as a fair and honorable person because I think of myself in those terms. That kind of sincerity is hard to miss. This is the only way I know how to negotiate. I truly believe that if I establish that I am trusting and trustworthy, my negotiating partner will respond in kind.

34. Seek His Unique Problem

This is the flip side of what I've just suggested. You should want to know the other side's special problems. If you attempt to discover them, you can only create an atmosphere of trust. You might even be able to satisfy his unique problem and still come out ahead.

There are no tricks to finding out the other side's unique problems. Just be direct. Is the company going to be taken over soon? Does he have a new boss? "Tell me the truth, is something bothering you?" I'll even ask, "Can I be of help to you?" Or, "Are you having trouble with the new owner?" "Do you have a budget problem?" "Are the partners bickering with each other?" "Will you be in jeopardy if you don't finish this by tomorrow?" "Is there anything I should know that would be helpful?"

Believe me, this approach accomplishes several goals. One, it makes the other person a bargaining partner, not an adversary; two, it gives me a little more information that helps me frame as beneficial a deal as I can, given the other side's special circumstances.

35. Keep a Secret

Just as important as it is to gain someone's trust, don't violate it. If, in the course of the negotiation, your opponent confides in you, keep his secret. Don't violate the trust and tell others some private information. That will serve to hurt your reputation and severely damage any future negotiations with the person you've hurt.

If people ask you not to say anything and you stand by your guarantee, you build a reputation as someone who is trustworthy. This can give you an advantage where people will tell you things they won't tell others, an edge that can yield important information for you.

I frequently tell this joke: Someone asks me if I can keep a secret. I say, "Sure, *I* can. It's the people I tell who can't!"

36. Don't Give Information, Try to Get Information

Just because you are making your presentation doesn't mean you can't ask questions. On the other hand, they will probably be questioning you, too, and you want to give up as little information as possible unless it benefits your case. Avoid saying anything that weakens your position.

For example, even during your presentation you might ask them if they have any kind of cost breakdown of their offer (yearly salary, bonus, incentives, etc.). Clearly, this would be helpful to you. On the other hand, you will want to avoid giving them a breakdown of your costs unless you think the figures help your case.

Don't be afraid to ask questions. Some people think it's intrusive or an invasion of privacy to ask questions. It's not. Asked politely, a question is not offensive. Just be careful not to make your inquiries seem like an interrogation.

But for your own protection, you risk giving up valuable information if you volunteer it. If they ask, give as little (or as much) as you think necessary or possible. If you remember to ask all the important questions, you will have less heartache later.

Remember, you are looking for whatever edge you can get, which means not relinquishing any edge you have.

37. Appraise Both Positions

You have already appraised your opponent's position after his presentation. You assessed your leverage after hearing what was offered. Now you've made your presentation and you must now take a step back, breathe deeply and appraise both positions. It can take a few minutes, an hour or a day. But you need time to regroup and analyze. Don't be forced into making an immediate reply, even if you're ready to do so.

Ideally, you'll have plenty of time to sit down and think both sides through. But many times, you will get a response or even a counteroffer the moment you finish talking. In that case, you *must* try to take time at the end of your proposal to digest whatever has happened on both sides.

When you've received that immediate response from the other side, don't respond right away. I'll frequently say, "I'll see what I can do," or "I'll talk to my client and see how he or she feels."

Think before you act. Appraise both positions. Then appraise them again.

38. Make Sure the Other Side Knows You *Want*, but Don't *Need* a Deal

A negotiation is rarely a do-or-die situation, just do-or-don't. Make it clear that you (or your client) would *like* to have a deal, but you can live without one. There is a world of difference between the two atti-tudes. If he knows this is a deal you absolutely must have, expect to be shown little mercy. Of course, if you in any way can determine that he can't survive without the deal, that would be to your obvious advantage.

Whenever somebody says he's willing to do what's necessary to sign one of my clients, I feel more confidence and leverage is on my side. When Donald Trump was talking about signing Doug Flutie to play for his USFL New Jersey Generals, he said publicly that he'd pay "a reason-ably ridiculous amount" to sign Doug. Outwardly, I was calm. But inside, I was saying, "Great!" because I knew, then, that I had the opening to ask for a justifiably high contract and come in on the higher end of my own estimates.

Showing that you *need* a deal weakens your bargaining position, and will result in your selling yourself short in salary, selling your house for less than it's worth, or paying more for a car because you're desperate to have it. The other side will sense this weakness and pounce on you.

Be cool and consistent emotionally. Never get overly enthusiastic. Tell your opponent, "That's a nice offer. But I think I'll sleep on it," not "I'd love it." Showing that you *need* it, will almost always yield a better deal for the other party.

When it's all over, *then*, you can show your enthusiasm.

39. Be Flexible—Have an Open Mind To Everything

Negotiating demands subtle shadings and a supple mind. Examine your flexibility. The ability to adjust quickly to new and perhaps unex-pected information is vital. Without the capacity to give and take you are not a negotiator, you are just there. If you find yourself in no mood to listen, react, or adapt, you should not approach the table at all, step away from it, or concentrate on changing your state of mind.

If you are inflexible you will get either exactly what you want or absolutely nothing. And since people rarely achieve that perfect goal, you are setting yourself up for failure. I cannot overemphasize this. Be flexible. Invent situations and try to find solutions to them which are consistent with your overall goals.

40. Prepare Giveaways

Negotiation is entirely a game of give and take, and it is vital in preparing to do business that you take an inventory of your bargaining possessions. These are always "add-ons" and "take-offs." Even the old horse traders tossed in a blanket now and then or took off a bridle as the deal began to take shape.

I always try to have several peripheral issues to raise, things I would like to include but could live without, as an inducement for protecting what I consider the heart of the contract. If I get these fringe requests, so much the better. But, if I have to discard them, I do so one by one, and very slowly, so that the other side will appreciate the fact that I am compromising, that I am not winning every point nor getting everything I ask for—and neither should he.

Your giveaways should be enumerated on the list of items you've included in your proposal. You rarely ever win everything that you want in a negotiation, and being able to give away a few things you don't need creates some goodwill and also creates the opportunity for the other side to do the same.

There are plenty of giveaways found in everyday negotiating: you'd like whitewall tires thrown in free with your car; you'd like the furnishings in the house you're buying at minimal extra cost; or you'd like a company car to go with the job. But if these extras prove detrimental to completing the deal, you can get rid of them. You didn't *need* them, you only wanted them. They were expendable, but still worth asking for.

41. Have Numerous Acceptable Alternatives Prepared

This is a measure of the fact that you have done your preparation and looked at the problem in many different ways. When you are actually in the negotiation, you must have several suggested solutions based on information you may have gleaned in your discussions. You always need a fallback position. This is your chance to be creative in anticipating what kind of problems may arise.

The alternatives must be things you can live with in place of getting what you originally wanted. The alternative may not be the original, but it's still beneficial. Say you ask for a raise and you're told that the company isn't giving any this year. Rather than just being disappointed, you've thought ahead and you're ready with alternatives: Can I get my parking paid for? A clothing allowance? Payment for educational advancement? An extra week of vacation? Or set up a retirement plan?

It is important to note that you're not just dreaming up alternatives. If you had a $5,000 raise in mind, you have thought through what that would be worth to you in benefits. If the figure can be justified, then the answer might be a combination parking and clothing allowance.

You might want to buy a business, which is valued at $1 million. But you don't have all that financing up front. How about paying the money over four years, which will provide the buyer with a steady income and a lower tax bite?

42. Show That Other Choices Are Worse Than Your Proposal

As a negotiating tactic, Henry Kissinger always made every other choice less attractive than the plan he originally suggested. With each new argument, you actually reduce their options. In the 1970s, if a European country was unwilling to agree to a greater increase in American defense missiles within their boundaries, Kissinger did not turn to forceful measures. Instead, he would discuss the alternative choice of *not* increasing American missiles, pointing out that the surrounding countries would then be militarily stronger and make his negotiating partner's country more vulnerable to attack in the future. In this way, Kissinger enabled his negotiating partner to see the advantages of agreeing to his proposal.

43. Keep a Record of Each Conversation

When you're negotiating, you'll want to keep track of what's going on. In that case, you will need notes, memos, a good record of each conversation or meeting. Few people do, and, when reminded of their past positions, they fumble around and lose points. Having the facts is a basic part of the preparation we described earlier; keeping track of them is just as important.

I jot down ideas and numbers while I am working, especially when I am negotiating over the telephone. I summarize the tone or final positions of *that* conversation as soon as it ends. I keep these notes filed and organized. My office is my own reference library.

Many business people juggle conversations and conduct several unrelated negotiations at one time. A busy executive may pass his incomplete notes to his legal department to be drafted into a contract, but the lawyers may not know the correct figures. Good notes will prevent a potentially nasty foul-up. The first time you forget one important point in a deal, you will appreciate the benefit of notetaking.

Once, I was negotiating the contract of a television meteorologist and the harried station manager said to me, "I'm never going to give you more than $120,000." I knew the market, knew the station could do better, so I decided I could afford to be patient and persistent. Just before we hung up, he repeated himself: "I'm telling you, under no circumstances will I go beyond $120,000."

I called him back two days later. "Under no circumstances," he repeated, "will I go beyond $120,000. That's it."

I called back again at the end of the week. "Why are you still calling me?" he snapped. "I told you, my best offer is $120,000. That's it."

Now I waited two more weeks. "Bob, you're wasting your breath," he said. "I told you, *$140,000* is as far as I'm going to go."

It was almost comic, but true. The man had been wading through an unusually hectic month and had failed to write down the figure. My notes were better than his. As a result, my client's salary was greatly improved.

44. After Each Conversation, Reassess Your Leverage

Terms and positions may change frequently during the course of negotiations. People may get caught up in emotional reactions to each change. They forget that any negotiation is an exercise in give-and-take. Where you stand at any particular point in the discussions doesn't mean that's where you'll be when talks conclude.

Remember to stay tuned to the situation, not your hurt feelings. While you're busy nursing grudges, you may lose sight of the fact that the situation has subtly changed. If increased leverage comes your way unexpectedly, you want to be prepared to recognize it. You won't be able to make use of it if you don't realize it's there.

Reassess your position with respect to leverage after each conversation. Does the other side want to make a deal more now than they originally did? Are they more desperate? Less desperate? I have had numerous occasions where I've tried to get a team to sign a backup quarterback, with no luck. But by mid-negotiation, the conversations have changed radically when the starting quarterback got injured or sick. Suddenly, my client was in demand and valuable to the team.

Remember, leverage is the game: you've got to *keep* score.

45. Come Up or Down Slowly

Now we're into the actual bargaining phase of the negotiation. My experience has been that you want the other side to earn whatever it is getting. Basically, this means coming up or down slowly. If you have to make dramatic jumps in what you want or are offering, it means your initial position was either way off or you risk sending a signal to the opposing party that you don't know what you are doing.

It isn't all that important to me what they may be doing. If they make a dramatic change, fine, but we will stick to our course. As a practical matter, it just works better if you move slowly, prudently, and with care.

Make them grind it out. If you're coming down in your requests, come down slowly and with reluctance. Just because they want you to come down quickly doesn't mean you have to do so. By changing your position slowly, you've given the other side a sense of accomplishment, that you're coming down and they're earning little victories. You may eventually get down to the level your opponent wants, but you may not. By immediately leaping to what your opponent wants, you're giving in immediately. That's *very* bad negotiating.

46. Never Raise or Lower a Price Before You've Been Asked To Do So

Some people act on impulse. Either out of eagerness or insecurity, they will state a figure they want. Then, before the other person can even blink, they change it! Just blurt out a new number. Why would anyone do this? It has always seemed strange to me. It isn't very smart. It is usually the insecurity or a fear of the process that will cause them to suddenly change their minds.

It's amazing how many people voluntarily do this. Sometimes, you ask, "How much are you asking?" The other person says, "I was thinking of $100,000, but if necessary, I'll take $80,000." Why lower a price when you haven't heard the offer? You'll always have time to raise or lower a price. But do it when you're asked, not in anticipation of being asked.

47. Don't Give Tit for Tat

The idea here is that if they come up fifty, you are not obligated to come down by fifty. Just because they're making an adjustment by a certain figure, you are under no pressure to respond with the same amount. Don't feel you have to make a concession every time the other side does. You are not obligated to follow their lead. They may have started out too low and can afford to look generous in raising their offer. You may be reasonably close to a number that represents a fair settlement. You simply have to analyze this action and not get caught up giving tit for tat.

If my opening bid for a product is $100 and my opponent's is $60, and he goes up to $70, there is no reason for me to go automatically to $90. Rather, I'll drop, if I feel I must, to $95. This may exasperate the other side, or it might also please him to know that he's forced me to concede a little bit.

Not only do you *not* have to reduce your bid by the same amount the other side is increasing its offer, you don't necessarily have to make any move at all. When I'm faced with this situation, when I feel I'm at my bottom line, I'll say, "I'm sorry, I feel I'm at a fair price. Can you make your offer a little better?"

48. Don't Split the Difference

This is a major point. Let's say that I'm asking $100,000. Your offer is $75,000, and eventually, you say, "What the heck, let's split the difference and call it $87,500." From seeing this happen frequently, my advice is not to accept the offer, but in a nice way.

In my experience, in most negotiations, somebody will say, "Look, in order to get this over with, let's just split the difference." It happens so often that many people consider this to be almost a rule of trade. Rather than just agree and be done with it, as nine out of ten people will do, this is the point where I say politely, "I can't split the difference, but I will do this . . ." And your move is to come back only part of the way, like "May I suggest $95,000?" or "I can't go down to $87,500, but I'll make it $95,000." The fact is, you *already* have his figure. He just offered it to you. That money is on the table. You can always come back to it later on if you don't handle it unpleasantly.

Don't snap at the bait, no matter how tempting it may be as a way to get nearly all you want and to end the negotiation. Be a smart negotiator and you will earn a little more without offending anybody.

49. Check Their Real Concerns vs. Your Position

For every important position the other side takes in a negotiation, they are going to have certain reasons, or concerns, that would make clear why they took them. If you can ask questions to help you understand these positions, you can eliminate those concerns and arrive at solutions favorable to you. What they are saying publicly may be colored by a much more private concern. Discovering that concern may make the negotiation go much easier.

Once I was seeking a no-cut contract for a player so he would be sure to receive all the money we were trying to obtain for him. The team rejected the request out-of-hand. Their position was that they would not give any no-cut contracts.

After some additional probing, I learned that their fear was that they did not want a player taking up space on the roster who could not make the team. They were actually not that concerned about the money. We resolved it by having them guarantee payment according to the contract terms whether he was on the team or not.

50. Check His Perspective—He May Be Right

As a professional negotiator, I was hired by the City of Boston to bring in the top entertainment talent in the country for outdoor summer concerts in the Boston Commons park. For the first time, I was on the buying end, hiring talent instead of selling it.

Very quickly, I was amazed, not only at the amount of money they were asking, but by their special demands. I started negotiating with the managers of Whitney Houston, Patti Labelle, John Denver, Liza Minnelli, Willie Nelson, Kool and the Gang, and Luther Vandross, and what I found stunned me: demands for dressing rooms of a certain size and color, stocked with a certain brand of wine and hot food, with instructions on how it should be prepared. The food had to be served on fine china, with a linen tablecloth, sterling silverware. My reaction was, "You have got to be kidding!"

It all came under the heading of "hospitality" and my client, the City of Boston, was expected to pick up the tab. I was disturbed by the mentality that I thought existed here, until I began to look at it from the celebrity's perspective, which was later confirmed by my experiences with the New Kids on the Block.

In representing stars who earn $100,000 to $250,000 a night, I also would want them to work under the very best conditions possible. All the requests they make grow out of bad experiences the performers had on the road. In the interest of my client, I would want them to be comfortable. If a performer is on tour, they are most likely in a different city every other day. All of a sudden the request that the dressing room be painted purple didn't seem so outrageous. I could see that their managers wanted as many things as possible to be familiar to their performers, so they would feel relaxed and comfortable before their shows to ensure their best possible presentation to the thousands of waiting fans. I wouldn't want them to fly into town and encounter a series of shocks, big or small.

I would want them to have really good food, nice dishes, and real tableware. There is a delicate chemistry involved when you deal with performers. And I realized that if I were representing *them*, these are the things I would be insisting upon. I would want to know that they had the right kind of electrical outlets and all were working. I would want them to feel totally secure as much of the time as possible during their stay in each city.

Remember, always try to put yourself in the other person's shoes. Think of why he is making these requests and whether they are *truly* excessive or practical in terms of the product or service he is delivering. Give the other person's viewpoint credence.

51. Be Optimistic and Give Them Encouragement

This is a continual task you will have throughout the negotiation. I have always found that being upbeat and taking a positive attitude throughout the process—repeating "We *will* make an agreement. It will be good for everybody"—makes the other person respond in the same way. By creating and perpetuating this kind of atmosphere, you reduce the risk of reaching an impasse or having the talks break down.

You must keep doing it, even if negotiations seem to be faltering. As I've said before, there are few negotiations that can't reach a satisfactory conclusion. And even if you've reached a brick wall and you have to depart without a deal, leave with encouragement, too, by saying, "I'm hoping we can come back soon and work on this deal again."

52. Check Your Emotions—Never Get Too High or Too Low

All negotiations begin at ground zero, and any emotion from outside sources, or a carryover from a previous success or failure, may unnecessarily color this new situation. The best view is a consistent one. Stay on an even keel. Don't let a victory make you cocky or a defeat crush you. The whole process begins again so often, you must be able to renew yourself as well. You constantly have to evaluate your emotions and keep a balance. If you are unnaturally giddy or solemn, you're doing damage to yourself. If you are too high emotionally, you may not be able to shift gears when circumstances change in a negotiation. Sometimes they change very quickly. Things can go wrong in the blink of an eye and you don't want to be caught off-guard while celebrating prematurely.

If you maintain your even temperament you can keep a better check on your attitude throughout the negotiation. Are you feeling frustrated, angry, or depressed? Personal matters may be going wrong for you away from the negotiation. Are they draining you of your optimism about meeting your goal? If you are not constantly watching yourself and keeping your emotions in check, all the hard work and sound principles you have tried to apply can go down the drain. If you don't keep a firm grip on your emotions and your attitude, you are more apt to make bad judgments for yourself or your client.

53. Don't Negotiate When You Are Tired

When you are tired, you are less willing to maintain a solid stance, your resistance is down and you are irritable and sometimes irrational. Problems grow and become more serious when your body and your mind are exhausted. So don't react to any situations when you are in this state. This is putting yourself at a disadvantage, and there are enough pitfalls and problems in a negotiation without creating additional ones.

Be on guard against attempts to negotiate when you are less than alert. Years ago, when I flew into Japan with Carl Yastrzemski to discuss various business opportunities there for Carl, our Japanese host tried his hardest to whisk us right from the plane to our hotel so we could begin negotiations. They knew what they were doing. We were tired. They were at their best and hoped to get the best deal for themselves.

Common sense will tell you that when you're tired, you are not going to make the most rational decision; you're likely to give in or miss an important detail. Take a break. Call a time-out. Get a decent night's sleep and return to the negotiating table well-rested.

Remember what Vince Lombardi said: "Fatigue makes cowards of us all in the fourth quarter."

54. Test His Concentration

People get tired and run down. They have other things on their minds. As meetings rock along, you may think, "I'm really making some strong points and doing everything right. But the other party doesn't even seem to be listening to me."

In truth, the attention span of most people is rather short. A rule of thumb in television is that no story can run longer than three minutes with one person staring into a camera without the audience growing bored or restless. The success of MTV and such publications as *People* and *USA Today*, is based on the belief that most of us no longer have much of a concentration level.

When you're talking, you don't want to have to ask, "Is this person listening to me? Am I wasting my time?" You are there to make a deal and if the other person is not focusing on you and what you are saying, then the negotiation will prove fruitless. If the other person is paying attention to some, but not all, of what you are saying, serious misunderstandings can result.

When I give speeches, I spice my words with a few jokes. Every few minutes, I try to make my audience laugh as I realize their attention may wander. This is the story I usually use to see if I'm keeping my negotiating partner's attention: When I was a guard for Boston College, our biggest rival was Holy Cross and their star was basketball great Bob Cousy. We played them six times, and in one game, I proudly state, I held Cousy to sixty-three points! If I get no reaction, I know they're not listening.

55. Satisfy Your Partner's Need to Earn or Accomplish Something

After all these years, I believe I know human nature. I've observed that if anything comes too easily, people are skeptical or dissatisfied. They have a need to feel they earned what they received, that they worked for it.

They are suspicious if the payoff comes too quickly. If you wanted $100,000 for a house, how would you react if I said, "Sold. I'll take it." The thought immediately explodes in your head: "Oh no, I should have asked for *more.*"

But let's say I offered $75,000 and you said no. You say no at $80,000 and then $85,000, and finally we meet at $90,000. In all likelihood, you will feel better accepting that figure than you would the $100,000 I gave you a moment ago. You worked for it. You feel you *earned* it. This is human reality.

Or an employee asks the boss for a $5,000 annual raise. Immediately, without batting an eye, he says, "Fine," and returns to the papers on his desk. I can almost guarantee that the employee will leave the office wondering if he shortchanged himself. I know that feeling. We all do.

That is just human nature. If your boss says he has to think about the raise and he takes a day to ponder it, and then says yes, your heart will leap like a fawn. It is strange but true. Always leave them, if you can, with a feeling that they accomplished something.

56. Don't Try to Tell Them How to Conduct Their Business

There is nothing worse than dictating to the other side how they should run their business. People do tend to resent being told what to do, especially if you are delving in their area of expertise. I have seen many negotiations fail because one party tried to tell the other what they should be doing or offering at a certain point in the negotiation. The other side will take umbrage at a statement such as, "From my calculations, you should be paying at least two dollars more a unit." Do you really know every factor involved in their decision process which helped them arrive at their offer? Probably not.

Instead of projecting what I think the other side should be doing, I discuss what seems to be the norm at that particular time, letting them know what I believe is the current market value. I might say, "The other companies have been paying in this range of figures for this type of situation." This gives the other side a chance to explain to me why their offer may not be in that range and prevents me from insulting them by trying to tell them their own business.

57. Brainstorm if Possible

Very often it can be beneficial to sit down with people you know and trust, experts in the area, associates in your office, a spouse or a friend, and explain where you are, talk through the problems and see what their reactions are. This is brainstorming—picking their brains. Don't be afraid to stop in the middle of a negotiation, take a break, and make a call if you feel the need to talk it out with someone else for a fresh outlook.

For instance, given the myriad opportunities and negotiations required for the New Kids on the Block, we have found it most helpful to brainstorm as a management team. The team is led by Dick Scott, and includes his attorney Mark Weiner, the attorney for the New Kids, Barry Rosenthal, John Dukakis and Randy Vataha from my office, and me. These meetings have produced innovative input and beneficial solutions that weren't apparent at first glance.

Usually, people will have all kinds of different suggestions. The value in this exercise is in hearing a variety of viewpoints, which may open new avenues of thought or add a little shading to your own conclusions. You may have overlooked something or missed something completely in the negotiations. During the negotiations, if you run into a roadblock or an impasse, brainstorming can be very helpful. It may even be crucial.

58. Keep Your Client Informed During the Negotiation

In representing a client, some people tend to think they are protecting the client by not keeping them informed about the ups and downs of the negotiation. They simply report that they have a deal, it's a good deal, and sign your name right here. My experience has been that the client needs to have an appreciation of what is happening, the good and the bad, what is being accomplished and what the problems are. In this way, you can pass on to them the same feeling of accomplishment you have as a negotiator.

Even if your client is not an experienced negotiator, he or she may have certain concerns that you should be aware of as a negotiation proceeds. He may feel you've gone as far as you should, asking for more money or more years or more guarantees is too much. As with your colleagues or family, your client may raise a point you overlooked.

59. Use Discretion When Keeping Your Client Informed

While it is very important to keep your client informed of your talks, use discretion in how you relay your conversations based on your evaluation of your client's temperament. Is he a stable or insecure person? Can he handle the criticisms that might come up during the process of a negotiation? Can he handle the lack of an immediate solution that may occur? If you give him a word-for-word rendition of your negotiation conversations, will it shake him up, make him angry, or lose confidence in himself? You need to properly read your client when you are relaying information to him. While you need to inform him of the essence of the conversation, you may want to soften some of the terms that were actually stated. For instance, "The company is not completely pleased with your performance at this time," instead of "They said you're a terrible employee!" Since your goal is to bring the two parties to an amicable agreement at a later time, it's important to always protect that future relationship by not alienating one party from the other by revealing opening arguments which are often presented in the extremes to justify a certain opening position. If you relay exact words, your client may take them too personally and never be able to forget them, even long after the negotiation ends.

60. Keep All of Your Client's Advisors Informed

If your client is the type of person who has close friends, family members, or longtime family advisors or mentors who have always helped him or her with decisions, and if your client has requested that they be involved in the negotiation process, make sure you take the time to consult them. Call each person and bring them up to date regularly so that no one feels alienated from the negotiation process. If your client is heavily influenced by these people, it can only help your negotiation if you have their total support.

61. Expect the Unexpected

I've had so many negotiations where the conversations were pleasant and everything was going smoothly, and the moment I mentioned money, the other party changed drastically. They either turned cold or a fierce look came over their faces or they simply came unglued.

Certain things set people off. When you are in a serious negotiation, the trick is not to be surprised by whatever reaction you get. Unfortunately, the process of negotiation changes some people, creating a Jekyll-to-Hyde transformation; nice people turn into terrors.

The general manager of a Los Angeles TV station is just like that. He can speak volumes about how much he loves my client, but the minute I mention the raise I expect him to pay, he gets angry. What do I do? I stay patient. I stay quiet. I ignore transgressions. I change the subject. I tell a joke. I take a break. When the subject circles back to the salary, the anger has usually subsided. Then we can proceed.

62. Check His Perception of Your Position

You need to be aware, and think about not only what leverage you actually have, but what resources he *thinks* you have that may emerge from your discussions. You are really trying to determine how strong he thinks your position is. You want to take advantage of whatever the perception is. Conversely, if you feel he doesn't fully understand the actual strength of your position, you need to be sure to elaborate and enlighten him, using whatever methods will demonstrate to him that you have the goods in those areas.

Remember, wars are sometimes won not by the armies you have, but by the armies he *thinks* you have. See if he actually understands you. If he *thinks* you're a great power, maintain the perception.

We ended World War II on the *perception* of having more bombs than we did and persuaded Japan of the perception, not the reality, of our atomic power.

63. Don't Let Them Intimidate You

Some people, by nature or as a tactic, will try to bully you. If they use this technique, it generally means they have gotten a reaction in the past that worked for them. Otherwise, they wouldn't be behaving in that manner. By not allowing yourself to be intimidated, or drawn into a shouting match, you can keep your focus on what you should be thinking about.

In most instances you can gain an advantage. When your opposition realizes you can't be intimidated, they usually run out of steam and become a lot more rational. But if you are goaded into reacting to the intimidation, your attitude and reasoning will change for the worse.

Intimidation does not happen all that much, but when it does, you have to be prepared for it. My best advice is to ignore bullying tactics until they lose their sting. That will happen. Just sit there. Nod. Smile politely. If it gets too bad, you might have to leave the room or hang up the phone. But don't show it's getting to you.

You may come across a Red Auerbach or George Steinbrenner-type in your negotiating. If you do, try this exercise: think of why the person is trying to intimidate you. What pressures are weighing on him? Is his boss being tough on him? Is he just naturally like this? This will separate the person from the issues you're negotiating and may give you the detachment necessary to ignore the aggressive tactics and move forward.

64. How to Deal with Ultimatums

In most cases, I have found that when people issue hard and fast ultimatums—take it or leave it; if you don't accept this condition, then everything is off—you are better off not making the deal.

Most ultimatums are artificial and are used only by the other side to try to gain an advantage, to intimidate you, or to bring the deal to a close in a preemptive way. Never let an ultimatum intimidate you. You simply must have the poise to continue the negotiations. In most cases, it will work out. If it doesn't, you are probably going to be better off.

I've dealt in numerous situations where an executive said to me, "Unless you sign the contract by 4 P.M., forget it." But the ultimatum was usually empty. I figured, if they wanted what I could give them at four, they'll want it at six and they'll want it at eight.

Or I've heard this: "If you don't take this, we'll take it off the table." Why did they say that? To force me into taking something quickly. I don't do that. But unless they had suddenly discovered someone who could easily replace my client in their plans, then the ultimatum was transparent and ineffective. Invariably, I ignore these kinds of ultimatums, and continue to negotiate.

65. Use Time Constraints Wisely

Timing is at the heart of every negotiation. The first step is to use the time constraints wisely. If a deadline is drawing near that works to your advantage, use it. If time favors the other side, don't let them use it to squeeze you. Look for creative alternatives to avoid having that happen.

A good example is the contract I was negotiating for Thurl Bailey, a top forward for the Utah Jazz basketball team. Despite negotiations up to the expiration date of Thurl's old contract, we couldn't agree with the Jazz on a new agreement. Rather than get forced into something that didn't make sense for Thurl, I was able to get the team's counsel, Phil Marantz, to agree that the new agreement would be retroactive to the date the current contract ended. When the contract was signed on a day in February, its provisions were retroactive to the previous November.

A deadline is simply the use of time to force an action. You should *never* allow the clock or the calendar to push you into an unwanted decision. That's why one of the most frequently heard phrases in labor negotiations is "Stop the clock." Despite the midnight expiration of a teachers' union contract, the city and union have agreed to keep talking past the deadline. Neither side was ready to sign a contract they weren't satisfied with and wouldn't let the time constraints overly influence their decision.

66. Creating and Dealing with Deadlines

Yes, the situation may require a deadline. The contract may have expired. His eligibility may be up. The availability of the product ends. But you don't want to make the deadline seem like a threat or coercion. "I wish I could have an answer by four o'clock. That's when my plane leaves for Europe. Who knows what might happen in the time I am gone?" or, "Two other people are coming in with offers, so I hope I have your answer by the end of business today." The result of setting a deadline in this unthreatening way may achieve the same result as being angry or aloof, but the other party won't have to feel that they were coerced.

Many deadlines are real and you have to respond to them by the time you are given. But sometimes deadlines are false. How do you tell? Analyze the deadline intelligently, with information you've dug up during your preparation: Have you approached the expiration date? Do you know independently that the product you want to buy will continue to be available after that date from another seller? From your analysis of the negotiation until now, ask yourself: Was the deadline issued in anger or was it proffered calmly? Is your opponent changing his mind or staying on course?

Analyzing a deadline by virtue of the facts behind it and the way it was presented can give you clues as to whether it is real or not. Negotiators will occasionally issue false deadlines to force the other side into action or force the other side into a better offer, lest the deal be lost. Some negotiators have such good poker faces that they can fool you into giving in to a false deadline. How many times have you been interested in buying a house and been told that there is another offer from someone else and you will have to make a commitment by the next morning or the house will be sold to someone else? Don't be pressured by deadlines.

Unless you are absolutely certain that you can't reach an agreement by a deadline, you should try to create a way to negotiate beyond the time limit. It's all in how you present yourself and your case for stretching the deadline.

67. Dealing with the Media

There will be times when the media will enter a negotiation. You'll be surprised what interests the press and how quickly they pounce on a story. A lot of people are afraid of the media, and that's understandable. They can descend in such large droves and can be so demanding that the immediate reaction might be to run and hide. Don't.

As we discussed in the leverage chapter, the media can be your ally. What if you're on the wrong side of the coverage? What if you have an unsympathetic client or a position that is viewed as unpopular? A lot of people think ignoring all press inquiries will make the problem go away. It won't. Because even when *that* negotiation fades into history, you may have to face the media again in the future, especially if your work generates a high profile.

When you're being tarred by the press is the time to be most available. Return the calls. Accept the lunch or dinner invitations. Be honest. Be available. Learn to talk off-the-record, where you agree to speak, but you can't be quoted by name on what you're saying, and you can be identified as a "source." Or speak on background, where you can't be directly quoted or used as a quoted source, but your information can be used to confirm or deny a point or as a building block for the reporter's story.

In both cases, be cautious about the reporter in whom you decide to confide. You have to feel comfortable enough with the reporter to trust him or her to preserve the terms of your conversation. When the media call, you should be responsive at the office and at home. Tell the reporter your "unique" problem that is making you handle the negotiation in an unpopular manner.

This will take up a lot of time, time that you might better put into work. But if your work takes you into the public eye, the media are part of your job. Just as you need to negotiate with a partner, you need to find time to negotiate with the media. *They* will always be there, and in the future, you may *need* them.

Remember, if your efforts don't yield a turnaround in the coverage of the negotiation you're under fire for, don't worry. Reporters will remember your cooperation and appreciate it. The next time around may be a lot easier.

In a typical day, my office logs 200 calls, many of which are from the media. I talk to all of them. It's time-consuming and sometimes even exasperating, but it also works two ways. A reporter may have a tidbit of previously unknown information for me. But if I don't cooperate with him, he might find an open door with my negotiating opponent, and I'd rather he get as much of his information as possible from me. Even if I've taken an unpopular position, my phone line is open to the media.

In essence, the media are another negotiating partner. Deal with them fairly and you will get your fair share of positive coverage—if it is deserved and if your position warrants it.

68. Take the Pressure off Your Client

Before the National Football League training camps opened in 1988, we were unable to reach an agreement with the Minnesota Vikings on a contract for Anthony Carter, their outstanding wide receiver. There was great pressure by the media on Anthony to sign because he was such an important part of the team.

In my public statements, I said, "Anthony Carter has put the decision in my hands. All he has asked me to do is to get him a fair contract. He is relying on my professionalism. Therefore, the fact that he hasn't signed yet is not a reflection on him, but rather a reflection on me."

When we were negotiating a contract for Larry Bird, and the Celtics charged that we were asking too much, I had to speak up. "Larry Bird isn't avaricious or greedy," I told the press. "*I'm* avaricious and greedy." They laughed, but it did take the pressure off my client.

You must protect your client and his reputation. That lives with him. When finishing work on a contract, make sure there is no animosity toward your client. The very best deal may be tarnished by bad press and public displeasure. If you're in my line of work, you've got to try to take the heat off your client. If someone is going to be publicly vilified, let it be you.

69. Protective Clauses

A good negotiator will anticipate that circumstances change and will build in clauses that offer protection or benefits in the event of a new situation. Even in the most modern of skyscrapers, with their mortar and steel and laser elevators, they still include fire escapes, don't they?

When negotiating for someone's services, you need to provide for what happens in the case of his death or disability. For the management's side, television talent contracts often contain morals clauses, allowing the station or network to fire an employee if his or her behavior offends community standards. There might be fifteen or twenty ways to terminate a contract for each side.

This applies to all kinds of situations. You may have put down a deposit on a house, but you want to be sure to get your money back if the house doesn't pass the inspection for plumbing or insect control. Protect yourself by putting that possible eventuality in writing in the purchase and sale contract agreement.

When I was negotiating Larry King's new contract with Cable News Network owner Ted Turner, I knew Larry might possibly go in for a heart bypass operation, so I negotiated a clause in the contract that he would need extra time off if he ever had a bypass operation. He'd get two months off, rather than one month for sick leave. As it turned out, he eventually went in for the surgery, and the clause was already in place in the contract, avoiding any misunderstanding regarding this benefit.

70. Preparing for Renegotiation

If people had the foresight during a negotiation to provide for a renegotiation, or the prevention of it, you would eliminate a lot of problems and acrimony. For example, if a quarterback starts a certain number of games, there is already a stipulation in the contract that his salary will be renegotiated. Or if the ratings of an entertainer's show exceed a certain level, the contract will be automatically eligible for renegotiation.

In the absence of a clause that triggers a contract adjustment, I have won for my clients a clause that provides for a "good faith" review after, say, two years. There are many ways to protect your client, or yourself, in the event of developments that make his or her services more valuable. The good negotiator is constantly planning for the future to get these clauses written into the contract.

71. In an Impasse, Change Something, No Matter How Minor

Head-to-head roadblocks do come up in the course of negotiations, and if you don't tear them down or find a way around them, they can bring an entire operation to a standstill. Solutions which are agreeable to all parties seem elusive, and there is often a moment when it seems fated that all will not work out.

Many times it is only because the parties haven't given their best attempt yet. In those cases, it just takes more creative thinking and flexibility on all sides to reach an agreement. "Let's think this through again and meet tomorrow," may be all that is needed to start the ball rolling.

Sometimes, however, all sides are stuck. Negotiators' gridlock. At that point, you stop looking for new avenues of approach and start searching sidestreets, anything to get you back on the main highway. Usually, it will be a minor point, just as long as it seems tangible.

When negotiations are stalled, frustrations rise, tempers overheat, and there is a real threat of a total breakdown in communications. I have found it helpful to make some kind of movement, any kind, just to reintroduce the sense of progress. Is there an auxiliary issue we haven't discussed? Maybe by demonstrating our ability to agree on a minor point we can approach the major one with fresh eyes. Maybe a concession on the new point can be tied to another, and that may be the force to break the logjam.

And you'd be surprised how different things look when that small point is reached. It's like finally finding the way out of the forest. Two sides could be squabbling, then a change is made, and both sides breathe a sigh of relief. Pretty soon, they forget what the fight was about.

72. Try Not to Give in on Important Issues

Obviously, there are important issues and lesser ones. You always want to try to hold firm on important issues and not be caught in the trap where the other party makes a minor concession, expecting you to yield on a major one.

In fact, I try to be the first to say, "I'll do this" (concede on a lesser issue), "if you'll do that" (give in on an important point). Sometimes it works.

73. The Favored Nation Clause

This clause refers to a standard payment or treatment accorded to multiple parties. It is effective not only among countries—where one country accords favorable tariffs to certain countries, for example—but in dealing with big egos where you want to avoid arguing about who is more important or more valuable: the politician, the sports figure, or the entertainer.

In representing your company, it can be a very worthwhile clause to avoid friction. If everybody is paid the same price or fee for the same service, all egos are satisfied. There are no arguments over who gets more. In the famous series of the "Do you know me?" American Express commercials, each celebrity received a standard fee of $10,000. No negotiation was needed and it prevented any second-guessing about stature or popularity.

74. Funny Money

Funny money is anything you think of as not being *real* money, even though it is! This psychology is clear to you the first time you ever leave Las Vegas and the cells in your brain unlock. They give you smooth chips instead of cash so you won't feel as though you are losing hundred-dollar bills like monopoly money.

When people travel in foreign lands, they don't think they are spending as much because the currency is unfamiliar to them. This is especially so when the exchange is heavily in favor of the American dollar and a few dollars go a long way.

There are unlimited ways to make funny money work for you in a negotiation. I will often defer some of a client's money, or postpone payments, which generally pleases the other side. At the same time, though, I'm getting interest compounded annually on that deferred amount and that can end up being more valuable than the salary being paid right away.

In short, there are many times when the company may not think it is giving up much, but the long-range benefit to you can be substantial.

75. Watch His Negotiating Tactics

Always be aware of what the other person is doing. Think in terms of the boxer who starts out in a right-handed stance and in the fifth round comes out of his corner, and approaches his opponent in a southpaw stance. If you haven't paid attention, you can get knocked out. It's exactly the same in negotiating.

Has the other side's attitude changed? Is there a radical shift in his logic, in his stubbornness, in his temper? Maybe he's playing head games with you. Maybe he's getting too aggressive. You need to observe what is going on, in order to anticipate the next move and protect yourself. Otherwise, you just may find yourself KOed.

It is safe to say that the other side will be working just as hard as you are to get what they want, so you need to be aware of their tactics all through the negotiation. Their moves may range from the reasonable to the ridiculous. Try to be ready for all of them.

76. Incentives for Them

This requires that you be creative. Incentives for *them* may involve opportunities outside the contract.

There are all sorts of incentives that you can offer in everyday negotiations: if you get paid a certain salary to come aboard a new company, you bring in a lot of clients the company has coveted; if you convince an opponent to settle an insurance claim for the price you want, then major trial costs are eliminated; and if you are able to pay me the price I am asking for by Friday, you will be able to avoid an upcoming price increase imposed by the manufacturer.

77. Whenever Possible, Get It Guaranteed

Obviously, in any contract, the more terms you can get guaranteed, the better off you are. But you have to make certain that the person, or entity, providing the guarantee is substantial and can actually fulfill that obligation.

I have been involved with many players who signed contracts with expansion leagues like the American Football League, the American Basketball Association, the World Hockey Association, and most recently, the United States Football League. Whenever possible, I insisted on the personal guarantees of the owners. Many other players had contracts guaranteed by the teams, and they were left holding the famous empty sack when the leagues went out of business. The owners were personally in far better financial shape than the teams they ran.

You have to make sure that the guarantee is backed by something, or someone, substantial. In the case of the USFL, billionaires like Donald Trump and Alfred Taubman could well afford to pay the salaries that they had personally guaranteed.

78. Be Patient—Especially if He Loses His Patience

If my negotiating partner feels a need to scream and yell, I let him. If he wants to tell me that my client doesn't deserve what I'm asking for, I let him. I listen. I find that once he's had a chance to get that pure rage out of his system, we can settle down and ultimately come to an agreement. Remember, hearing someone out doesn't necessarily mean you agree with them.

This example comes to mind. At one point during my negotiations for all-star guard Byron Scott with Jerry West, the general manager of the Los Angeles Lakers, West became extremely agitated. We had been negotiating for several months and West had finally offered to raise

Byron's salary from $600,000 to $1 million dollars annually for five years. I felt that the market could bear paying Byron $1.1 million per year. That extra $100,000 per year had Jerry hopping mad. He thought $1 million was fair and was outraged that I was asking for more. I was willing to hear him out, but I hoped in the end to make it clear as to why I thought the extra $100,000 was fair. But again, Jerry thundered, "I will not go over $1 million a year, I will not pay a salary over $1 million a year!"

I was surprised that Jerry had lost his patience because he is a genuinely kind man who is well liked by everyone who knows him, but it was clear he had reached his limit on this point.

"I see what you're saying," I said, trying not to counter his argument while he was obviously angry. We kept talking. I had to be patient and give Jerry time to calm down. I veered the conversation away from the issue of the salary and let the conversation drift toward more comfortable terrain: mutual friends, Magic Johnson, last night's game, whatever it took to break the tension. Not only did I give Jerry some time to cool down, I also afforded myself with some time to package my needs differently and in such a way that would be more palatable to Jerry's way of thinking. Instead of sticking to my request of $1.1 million a year, I told Jerry that I could understand his concerns about going over $1 million a year in salary and reduced my annual salary request to $1 million. I then discussed further with him the outstanding job that Byron was doing for the Lakers night after night and asked Jerry if he would consider giving a player of Byron's calibre a $500,000 signing bonus. I reasoned that a signing bonus would allow me to get the overall financial payments I was looking for, but would also accommodate Jerry's basic discomfort with going over a million dollars a year for a player. That type of structuring appealed to Jerry and we were able to come to an agreement.

Instead of matching Jerry's anger, I remained calm and patient and we were able to move along without any animosity.

79. Make Sure You Understand the Terms

While you are negotiating, you can *never* take for granted that you are both talking about the same point. This is not as obvious as it may seem. I have dealt with the film industry, the radio and television industry, all four major sports, in real estate ventures and in mergers and acquisitions. It has been my experience that not only does the language differ between the industries, but even within all of them, people do not always use the same definitions or meanings.

One of the first things I learned about the film industry was that you never agree to take net income *after* expenses, because, by definition, you can never make money, as quite often excessive production and business costs eat into profits, creating a loss even if millions in revenues have come in.

In any of these businesses, you will hear people talk about the net net, the gross net, and the gross receipts. In most industries, if you talk about an option clause, it usually means—unless specified differently—an option for either side. In sports, almost always an option clause deals with only the club having an option on the athlete's services. The option is not mutual.

The moral is, make certain you are speaking the same language. It can solve a lot of potential misunderstandings. If you're not sure how your opponent is defining something, ask. If you think the other side has a vague or mistaken idea of what you are suggesting, explain it. You don't want a misunderstood clause to come back and haunt you a week or a year later.

80. Don't Be Afraid to Say, "I Need Your Help"

There is a radical strategy that on occasion works wonders. It is called admitting you just don't know.

These are times when having established a mutual trust is a major point in your favor. A good negotiator will have prepared for this moment and be able to say, "Look, I am at your mercy. All I ask is that you please treat us fairly."

Fair people appreciate honesty and will respond favorably. It is not a disclosure you would make while dealing with people of questionable integrity; of course, you would be aware of their character and be prepared to try other tactics. You have to use extreme care and judgment when deciding to attempt this approach.

But when I feel the trust, I'll ask for help. You may be in an area in which you are unfamiliar with standard practices. Or you may not understand something completely. When I'm stumped or out of my element, I'll say, "Listen, I could use your help here. Treat me right. If you don't, I'll eventually discover if you were not being fair to me."

When the Music Corporation of America wanted to use the likeness of Gene Shalit on one of its video cassettes, they contacted me to negotiate a fee. This was a field in which I had little experience—hardly anyone did—and a true fair market value was unknown to me.

Sounding out MCA, I started talking amiably to the man who had contacted me, Ted Schmidt. He told me at one point during our talks that he had attended the University of Michigan. Groping for common ground, I mentioned that Bo Schembechler, the Wolverines' football coach, was a friend of mine. That struck a chord. Schmidt was a loyal Michigan fan and knew Schembechler as well. We both warmed to the conversation.

Finally, I said, "Ted, I'm at your mercy. Please tell me the very best you can do." The gesture is unconventional enough to bring a reaction that borders on sportsmanship. Most of us, at one time or another, have been in this spot and know the anxiety of being on the hook.

Schmidt and MCA were more than fair in their offer and Shalit called to tell me how grateful he was for my getting him such a good arrangement. In turn, the next time I deal with Ted Schmidt, I will try to act as responsibly as he did.

81. Make Sure He Doesn't Lose Face

Any time someone really embarrasses himself in a negotiation, the incident can be a deal-killer despite the merits of the agreement. It is one more thing you have to be aware of, so that you can try to avoid situations that will make the other side look bad to their client, other members of the team, their family or the public.

I'm reminded of the recent purchase of a 49 percent interest in Riviera Country Club, in Los Angeles, by a Japanese investor. The club's owner and the investor had been holding talks for several months, but the identity of the Japanese was not revealed throughout. All anybody knew was that a foreign investor was involved in the talks.

The secrecy bothered members of the club worried about the fate of the Riviera. The secrecy also stoked the interest of the press, which covered the story relentlessly, hoping to uncover the name of the investor. It wasn't until the final announcement that the investor became known.

Why all the secrecy? Well, the owner of the Riviera was abiding by the Japanese fellow's desires. If the public had known who he was and the deal had fallen apart in mid-negotiation, he would have lost face, especially back home in Tokyo, where he is a prominent businessman.

82. Be Prepared to Take a Stand

At some point in a negotiation—usually the tail end—you may be called upon to take a stand. You just feel the other side is being unreasonable and at that point no agreement can be reached.

When negotiating on behalf of John Bosa, an offensive lineman with the Miami Dolphins, the Dolphins' negotiating stance remained uncompetitive and unchanged. It was not advisable for John to report to training camp. As the season drew near, the pressure grew, so I flew to Miami to try to break the deadlock.

We wanted a multiyear contract worth $1.6 million. We were about $200,000 apart. I arrived amid some fanfare in the press, with pressure on both sides to get the team's first draft pick in camp. I met with head coach Don Shula and his director of player personnel, Charlie Winner, and nothing happened. They didn't budge from their last offer, and the next move was mine.

I decided I had to take a stand. I informed them that I was going back to Boston, with a one-day business stopover in Atlanta. I left Miami after announcing that Bosa would also be returning to Boston. This was uncharacteristic of me, to be the one to walk out on a negotiation, and I did so with regret. My flight from Atlanta to Boston was scheduled to depart at 1:30 P.M. At the airport, I received a message to call the Dolphins as soon as possible. But when I tried, no one was in.

At the airport, I bought a second ticket from Atlanta to Miami. I now had tickets on two flights, both on Delta, both leaving at 1:30, at adjoining gates, one to Boston, and one to Miami. I realized that if I used the ticket to Boston, it meant the negotiation was a disaster. Bosa would be a holdout for at least the first regular season game, a setback for John from a public relations point of view, and the very first time in my career that a client would be a holdout. However, I still felt I had to take that stand.

On the other hand, I knew that if I was called back to Miami by the team, I could be virtually assured of a deal. What I was not prepared to do was go back with hat in hand. I took my stand there, literally between the two cities, knowing what the consequences might be.

I felt like the star of a one-man morality play, torn between two gates, as if they symbolized success and failure, good and evil. Just before it was time to board, I reached Don Shula's office.

I said, "Look, I've got two tickets, one to Boston, one to Miami. Tell me which one to use."

The answer was, "Come to Miami."

We signed the contract that night. Bosa played in a preseason game that week and played well.

83. If You Have What You Want, Don't Let It Go Farther

As you go through the steps, and apply all the points, there will come a moment of truth, a moment when you have achieved all or most of your goals. After that time, things will deteriorate, and many people will begin to lose much of what they have won because they let the negotiation go too far.

It is difficult to pinpoint when this moment arrives, but you have to stay alert for it. One good rule is to pause after you have achieved most of your goals, and be sure you are not being too greedy. Keep asking, "Will it go downhill from here?" At that point, you can say, "Well, it looks like we've gone about as far as we can. Do you think we can wrap it up?"

If you feel there is a positive feeling in the air, and that more can be accomplished, keep going. But the instant you sense the momentum slipping away from you, bring the negotiation to a boil and get the agreement made.

84. Don't Be Afraid to Leave Something on the Table

There isn't any contract I have negotiated that I didn't feel I could have gotten more money or an additional benefit from. But don't feel you're going to get the last cent, because you're not. Nobody gets the last cent. That isn't what a negotiation is about. In fact, it's a very good negotiating tactic to leave something on the table. It leaves a better taste and it will show your lack of greed. The best negotiators I know do this consistently.

Sometimes that "something" can be very little, but it's still appreciated. Many years ago when my young daughters argued, the youngest, Tiffany, left something on the table.

223

When Tiffany was four and had a fight with her sister, Stacey, I made them kiss and make up. Afterward, Tiffany, clearly intending to get back in my good graces, said, "Daddy, I love you the *whole world.*"

I said, "That's nice. Now how much do you love your sister?"

I could see from the look on her face that her four-year-old mind was spinning. Finally, she said, "I love her the whole *neighborhood.*"

I was proud of her. This was Tiffany's way of leaving a little something on the table for her sister.

85. How to Handle the Nibbler, or the Hondler

You've just reached a mutually beneficial agreement and you're feeling great. The next day the phone rings and the person you closed the deal with asks you for "one more thing." He invariably "forgot" to ask you, or he claims that something else "has just come up." These people are known as nibblers, or hondlers, and they are *never* satisfied until they've gotten just a little more out of you.

Don't be afraid to say, "Look, we've both agreed on a very fair arrangement, and I would prefer to keep it the way it is." Most times, the nibbler will back off and feel that he has at least tried and you haven't been "hondled" into changing your original agreement.

86. Be Charitable

I try to instill the principle in all my clients that it is very worthwhile to give something back to society, not only in terms of the good they can do, but because there is such satisfaction in sharing their good fortune. I believe it is important for them to develop a social conscience and a charitable attitude.

Generally, I try to accomplish this by writing in a bonus clause based on my client getting so many sacks, or so many free throws, or the team winning so many games, with the money indexed for a good cause.

I also encourage them to establish a scholarship at their high school or college, and to set up a program to provide tickets for underprivileged children. If nothing else, I want them to get involved by contributing their time to a charity.

I also like to get the other side involved. One way to do this is to let them know you plan to give to charity the $500 for each sack your client will earn, then suggest, "Why don't you match it?"

If you are a businessperson or a salesperson, offer to make a contribution to a charity and ask your company to match it if you reach certain business goals on their behalf each quarter. This is more than a nice gesture. You enhance all relationships when you share your good fortune with society.

87. Never Make an Unauthorized Commitment

If you are representing someone, *never* make a commitment on behalf of your client without your client's full understanding and agreement to the terms of the contract. If you feel the terms are fair and are what you have been looking for on behalf of your client, you might indicate your own satisfaction with the terms by making clear to the other party that you agree with the terms, but state clearly that any official agreement is *subject to your client's approval.*

After a particularly long negotiation, I will give encouragement to the other side by saying, "I will be recommending this contract to my client, but the agreement is still subject to their approval."

88. Explain Any Agreement Fully To Your Client

Now that you've brought the negotiations to a final point of agreement, it is imperative that you take the time to ensure that your client fully understands and agrees to the terms. Make sure that financial terms; performance of services; options; guarantees; length of agreement; and all clauses, even if they are standard clauses, are fully explained to your client. I always ask my clients to *repeat* the terms back to me, so I can be sure that I have effectively relayed the information to them. This complete understanding by your client can help to avoid unintentional or inadvertent conflicts with the terms of the contract in the future.

CHAPTER NINE

What to Do After the Negotiation

Now THAT you have finally been able to reach an agreement and you are happy with the results, don't think your job is over. It's time to protect what you've prepared for and worked so hard to get.

89. Don't Oversell

Many a time, an agreement is reached and for no visible reason one of the parties won't stop talking about it, assuring the other side of what a good deal they've made. "You got a great deal here. No sir, no way to go wrong on this one." They go on and on, until the other side starts to get suspicious and the deal begins to unravel.

Once the deal is made, leave it alone. Don't talk it to death. Overselling it can only hurt, not help.

90. Before It's Signed, Keep It Quiet

In many instances, it is advisable to keep the agreement and its terms confidential because so many things can happen in the time between making the agreement and actually getting it signed. Many times the other side may not want others to know that they have come to an agreement with you. Perhaps they have other negotiations in the balance. By making your terms public, you may create outside pressure on the other side which could negatively affect their agreement with you. It is always best to inquire beforehand as to the level of confidentiality that is required at that time.

91. Reduce It To Writing

Once you have an agreement, both sides should sign a memorandum that states the basic, general points. I can't tell you how I felt the time I had a deal with someone, and we shook hands on it, only for one of us to look at the contract later and say, "Oh, wow, I didn't think you meant *that*."

The longer you wait to get it in writing, the greater the chance for misunderstanding, so do it right away. People might forget the terms agreed on. Maybe they'll want to sneak something in you didn't agree to if they think you've forgotten the little details over a period of time. So as soon as I've finished with a negotiation, I write a memorandum of understanding and send it to the other party as soon as possible. The sooner you get it on paper, the less room there is for a misunderstanding. Be sure both sides sign it.

92. Draw Your Own Contract

Whenever possible, you or your attorney should prepare the original draft of the contract. In every negotiation, people tend to focus on six, eight, or ten major items: how much is the money, when is it paid, over how many months or years. Naturally, if you are the one to draw up the contract, you will be sure to include all clauses that are favorable to you. Sometimes the other side will immediately agree to your version. This is preferable to you being the one who has to review the fine print in a contract prepared by the other side. Let the other party be the one who asks to make changes.

93. Some Lawyers Can Be Deal Breakers

I'm an attorney and I say this without prejudice: lawyers have to justify their presence. Since their role is to keep a client out of trouble, their instinct is to look for what can go wrong. They will build a worst-case scenario and pursue it until the participants begin to doubt that a deal can be made. The ones I know are not that bad. You may well need a lawyer; just keep in mind what their role is and do not let them make you paranoid.

I've heard it said by many people that when you work with lawyers in a negotiation, you have to remember that there is no course in law school that teaches them how to *make* deals, only how to break them. You need to keep that in mind before you rely entirely on an attorney's opinion.

How do you spot the deal*maker*? Look for one who doesn't trample on your ideas and keeps looking for the best ways to keep the process moving, not one who keeps seeking ways to kill the deal. Some lawyers have little justification for finding the gray clouds in silver linings.

94. Always Read the Entire Contract

This advice may seem to sound like those instructions on cellophane food wrappers that say, "Remove before eating." But it is remarkable how many people don't bother to read a contract.

Bud Adams, the owner of the Houston Oilers, tells an interesting story about his hiring of Bum Phillips as head coach. Bum had been on the staff of Sid Gillman, who moved up to the general manager's office and handpicked his successor.

When Adams called in Phillips to sign his contract, he was surprised when the rookie coach insisted on a clause that barred Gillman from the team's practices and meetings, and had his offices moved to another floor. "I'm a Sid Gillman fan," explained Bum, "but I won't have the respect of the players if he's around all the time."

Adams told Phillips, fine, put it in the contract and if Bum could get Gillman to agree, it was all right with him. And he smiled at the thought of the explosion he knew was coming.

The next day, Phillips walked in and handed him the signed contract. The surprised Adams asked how he got Gillman to accept his conditions.

"I just made the changes," he said, "and left the contract on Sid's desk. I don't think he ever read it."

95. Make Sure You and Your Client Have Exact Copies of Final Agreements for Your Files

Once the final agreement is signed, make sure your client has a fully executed copy of it for his personal files for future reference. If the agreement went through a series of amendments to the original document, make sure you have the corrected and final agreement in your files and marked as such in a prominent location on the document.

Don't completely depend on the other party to return the signed agreement to you. If you haven't received it within a reasonable amount of time, call or write to find out when you will be getting it.

96. Keep a Suspense File

Once you have finished negotiating a contract, stay aware throughout the life of the agreement of any particular timetables or special provisions. For instance, keep a reminder file as to when salary increases or increased ratings bonuses are to be paid; or when a window to look for other employment occurs toward the end of the contract; or when an option to renew notification needs to be sent in writing.

It's important for you to stay alert throughout the term of the agreement so you can protect the advantages you worked so hard to get in the first place.

97. Don't Second-guess Yourself

If you have done your work to the best of your abilities, be satisfied. Do *not* second-guess yourself. You will only inhibit yourself in future dealings. If you have given your fullest attention and effort, and performed to the peak of your ability, you have a right to feel satisfied no matter what the outcome. Don't deny yourself that pleasure. You will have earned it.

Even luminaries have doubts and anxieties, but they learn to control them and move forward. Leon Jaworski, the Watergate special prosecutor, argued before the U.S. Supreme Court to gain possession of Richard Nixon's secret White House tapes. In his book, *Confession and Avoidance*, he wrote: "I was not especially pleased with my performance. I felt a slight frustration, a letdown. I felt the flow of my argument had been lost. . . . Then I realized that I had never argued a case in which I did not wake up in the middle of the night, the next day or two, and wonder why I had failed to deal with certain issues or had overlooked points in my favor. The greatest arguments are always those that come to mind twenty-four to forty-eight hours after the conclusion of the trial."

In short, don't drive yourself crazy. You've done the best you can. Be proud of that. There is no need to give yourself ulcers. Enjoy your performance and go on to the next one.

98. Don't Be a Braggart

No matter how pleased you are with your agreement, be gracious. Don't gloat. Be generous or at least diplomatic, and contain your glee until you're back with your client or your colleagues. Don't brag all over town about your great deal. One very good reason for this discretion is the fact that you may not have the last laugh. Deals don't always turn out to be as good as you think, and you may wind up looking ridiculous.

Keep in mind one of the continuing themes of this book: you are building a reputation. You are here for the long term, and gloating can come back to haunt you the next time. Remember, you could be facing that person again in a month or a year. He'll remember your behavior.

99. Don't Ever Burn Your Bridges

If, for whatever reason you simply don't reach an agreement, you don't want to rush out and say rotten things about the other party, blaming them entirely for the breakdown. "It's their fault . . . they're unreasonable, unrealistic, impossible."

Sometimes, you may be *absolutely* right about the other side. But don't miscalculate your position in relation to theirs. You may be sitting across from those people again. They may have something in the future you will want very much. It is just poor business to criticize the other side and poison any future relationship you may have.

Show business is littered with people who fumed about their treatment by a producer or a network, stormed out, and found the pastures weren't much greener, then were blocked from returning to their previous position because of their extreme behavior. A far better technique when things go poorly is to show your dignity and say, "We didn't reach an agreement. There are reasons for it, but no useful purpose will be served by going into them." Try to part ways as amicably as possible.

100. Use Common Sense

All through the negotiation process, every step of the way, when in doubt, when you feel stumped by a situation that is either unexpected or provides several options, rely on your own, good common sense. This is one rule that is timeless and universal.

101. Keep Your Commitment

Once you've signed a contract, be prepared to live up to its terms. Be honorable. As we talked about earlier, stick to your convictions, don't give your word lightly, but keep it once you do. Don't go back and forth, adding or subtracting terms after the deal has been settled.

Nothing looks worse than someone backing out of a commitment. If you tend to have second or third thoughts, give yourself time *earlier* in the negotiation to handle them.

But some people are always angling and scheming to get out of a contract before the ink is dry. Be aware of them. Don't be one of them.

Negotiating Your Way Through Life

"Don't part company with your ideals. They are anchors in a storm."

—ARNOLD GLASGROW

"So live that you wouldn't be ashamed to sell the family parrot to the town gossip."

—WILL ROGERS

SINCE WRITING this book I have received great satisfaction from the response of many people who say they have utilized these suggested principles and have seen that my negotiating process really does work. I have heard from political figures, business executives, students, homemakers, and even relatives who have read excerpts of *Friendly Persuasion*.

My niece, Michelle, said she was disappointed with an 87 grade on a test. She went to her professor and explained quietly that she felt she had prepared thoroughly for the exam and had done a better job than the 87 grade would indicate. Michelle then asked her professor to reconsider her grade. He did and gave Michelle a 90, moving her up to an A grade. If Michelle hadn't asked, she never would have received the better grade. Principle: *It Doesn't Hurt To Ask.*

An interior decorator told me she had received an order of fabric that was defective. After making several angry calls, she still had not received any remedying response from the fabric company. Finally, after re-thinking her approach, she called back to say that she had been a satisfied customer of the company for many years and had always been pleased with their product and service. However, on this last order, she had been very disappointed with the quality of the product that had been delivered. The very next day she received a call from the customer service manager and the problem was resolved. Two principles: *Create the Proper Atmosphere and You Don't Have To Be Disagreeable To Disagree.*

I was in New York recently and a man approached me and said, "Thank you." I said, "For what?" He replied, "For the John Hannah story. I learned my lesson for the day from that. You can be sure that I don't lose my cool or get angry anymore in my business transactions." Principle: *Be Patient and Don't Get Angry.*

Several businesspeople told me they had applied the *Don't Split the Difference* concept and that they had ended up with more money than they had expected and everyone was still happy.

A corporate executive told me he came up *slowly* on his offer thus giving the seller a sense of accomplishment. The executive actually got his product for far less than he was prepared to spend, and again both sides were happy. Two principles: *Come Up or Down Slowly* and *Satisfy Your Partner's Need To Earn or Accomplish Something.*

Many of these principles and suggestions may seem basic, but you would be surprised how many people forget to follow what might appear to be obvious procedures. However, I have seen many negotiations fall apart for seemingly simple infractions: hurting the other side's feelings; lack of control of one's ego; attempts to intimidate the other side; and an inopportune comment. The list goes on. These are instances when the awareness of the basics would have saved the deal. Remember, as you get to the more sophisticated levels of negotiation, you must never forget the basics. The basics create the strong foundation upon which you build your negotiating prowess.

In the preceding pages, I have tried to guide you through all the levels of the negotiating process. I have explained the importance of creating the right atmosphere; being fully prepared at all times; watching what you say and how you say it; being gentle in your approach; being aware of your leverage and position at all times and the myriad techniques, strategies, and tactics; all to help you negotiate intelligently, as if you were playing a game of chess, thinking out each move, and preparing the next four moves ahead of time.

If you follow the basic precepts—treating people with decency and respect and never lowering your own standards—and utilize the suggested procedures in this book, you can be assured that you will be able to confidently negotiate your way through life and feel good doing it.